# Table of Contents

# INTRODUCTION

Inevitably when talking to knifemakers about their early struggles in learning to build functional yet fashionable knives, they say they eventually succeeded through trial and error, that there were no books on the subject at the time and few other makers in their area to help them. They plodded along on their own, being left to their own devices, and learned the hard way. It wasn't an easy way to make a living, and they nearly starved to death in the meantime.

While knifemaking remains a starving art, or at least a humble handcraft, there are continually more sources on the subject and resources available to help the novice maker succeed in the business. The Internet, knife magazines like *BLADE®*, books, knifemaking videos, even YouTube videos are easily accessed through the magic of online retailers and all other safe landing sites in cyberspace. If nothing else, a trip to Barnes & Noble or Books-A-Million will turn up a text that might answer a few of those nagging questions.

So what makes the *2nd Edition of BLADE®'s Guide To Making Knives* rise above the average instructional on building bladed beauties? The answer can be found not only in this completely updated, revamped edition with all new material, but in the first edition, as well. Sometimes finding the answers to questions that have long remained mysteries has less to do with the elusiveness of the information itself, and more to do with whom you ask. The Editors of *BLADE's Guide To Making Knives* have assembled an all-star cast of renowned knifemakers to bring you the most updated and exacting inside information on fashioning edged implements, period.

A designer and fabricator of modern, one-of-a-kind ornamental edged weaponry, John Lewis Jensen attended the Rhode Island School of Design, Savannah College of Art and Design and the Pont-Aven School of Art in France. He is an affiliate of the American Craft Council and the

Society of North American Goldsmiths. Prices for his knives often start at $10,000. His step-by-step illustrated chapter on fashioning "Desk Daggers: A Limited Edition Jensen Knives Trio" is one to which readers will instantly be drawn, leaving with the knowledge to embark on their own art knife journeys.

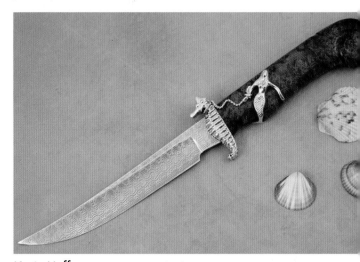

Kevin Hoffman

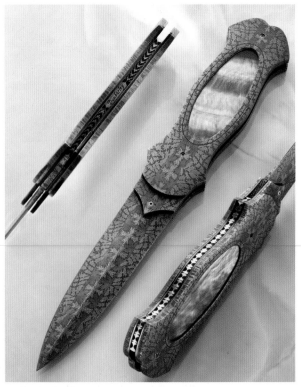

Rick Dunkerley

# BLADE's
# GUIDE TO
# MAKING
# KNIVES

## 2ND EDITION

### Edited by
### Joe Kertzman

Published by

Krause Publications a division of F+W Media, Inc.
700 East State Street • Iola, WI 54990-0001
715-445-2214 • 888-457-2873
www.krausebooks.com

To order books or other products call toll-free 1-800-258-0929
or visit us online at www.shopblade.com

ISBN-13: 978-1-4402-2855-1
ISBN-10: 1-4402-2855-8

Cover Design by Dave Hauser
Designed by Kara Grundman
Edited by Corrina Peterson

Printed in China

Tim Zowada, a respected full-time knifemaker who sold his first piece more than three decades ago, forges his own steel, including damascus and smelted steel, and specializes in working knives and straight razors. For the *2nd Edition of BLADE's Guide To Making Knives*, Zowada reveals his trade secrets and methods for "Making the Using Knife."

One of the world's most well-known knifemakers, Allen Elishewitz lent his knowledge and know-how to the book, authoring a chapter on "Making Patterns and Using a Pantograph" for those in the design stages of fashioning fine knives.

Add Don Fogg to the mix, arguably one of the best sword makers on the planet, not to mention a craftsman who fashions daggers, bowies and hunting knives, something he's been doing since 1976, and the book really starts to become interesting in his chapter on "Forging Steel from Raw Materials."

Vince Evans, who along with wife, Grace, crafts and embellishes Scottish dirks, Viking swords, Central Asian weaponry and other exotic and historical pieces, illustrates and writes about his methods for "Making and Carving a Scottish Dirk."

This is information readers will get nowhere else.

Continuing with a tradition of providing only the most valuable instruction on making knives, one of the "Montana Mafia" of renowned knifemakers, Rick Dunkerley, opens his world of knowledge to readers in a chapter about "Building a Damascus Locking-Liner Folder." Known for his mosaic-damascus masterpieces, Dunkerley and his works of edged art are crowd pleasers at knife shows and "hammer-ins" across the continent.

Specializing in distinctive folders and fixed blades, and a full-time knifemaker since 1981, Kevin Hoffman unlocks the mysteries of "Lost Wax Casting for Guards & Pommels," providing full-color images of each and every step of this tedious yet rewarding process.

No longer are budding knifemakers and enthusiasts left to stumble along blindly in dust-choked workshops experimenting with procedures that will inevitably fail, and then only to start again and repeat the same mistakes. With this, the *2nd Edition of BLADE's Guide to Making Knives*, readers will be on their way, armed with the knowledge necessary to reap the rewards of a fruitful and fulfilling knifemaking hobby or career.

Joe Kertzman
Managing Editor, *BLADE Magazine*
Editor of *Knives 2012*

Allen Elishewitz

Vince Evans

# Desk Daggers: A Limited Edition Jensen Knives Trio

## Introduction

Hello again fellow knife enthusiasts! It's been a few years since I've shared my working methodology with you here in this format. A lot has changed in terms of my approach since *Blade's Guide to Making Knives* was first published. Since the last edition, I've learned some computer rendering, embraced some CAM (Computer Aided Machining), moved studios twice, taken almost two years off from knife making, and outfitted my new studio with a ton of new tools and machines. It's been an exciting time and I'm glad to be back to share with you some of what I've learned. So, be prepared, as I'm going to pack a lot of knowledge and techniques into this format...

A couple of other things that I've done since the last book are to completely re-design my website, www.jensenknives.com, to reflect a higher-end and more modern design aesthetic, while also launching a corresponding facebook page, https://www.facebook.com/JensenKnives, where I share the behind–the-scenes aspects of Jensen Knives, including WIPs (Works In Progress) in real time and interacting with many of you answering questions and sharing my insights. For example, a more expanded version of the project I'll be sharing with you here in this book can be found over on my facebook fan page. In reality there are over 350 photos and even a few videos documenting the construction of these Desk Daggers. Due to the limited space in a book, I've had to really condense things, but I've done my best to show enough for you to fill in the blanks. If you'd like additional insight, so check out the facebook page. While these are simple knives as far as what I do, they are still

pretty complicated and none of these processes should be attempted without some basic metal working skills. So, I'm hoping and assuming that you have some knife-making experience already. Otherwise, you could really be in for a world of torture. The project I'm sharing with you here is an amalgamation of my classic goldsmith training, as well as my new-found skill set in CAD/CAM.

This project is a special first-time experience for me as well, as It's the first time I've done a limited-edition production run of one of my designs. I utilized CAD/CAM to cut all of the basic parts,

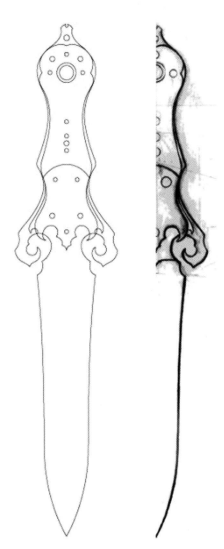

It all starts with the drawing. When designing symmetrical daggers, I only draw one half, I then continue to develop the design and make alterations by putting the drawing up to a mirror so that I can see what the overall piece will look like. This removes the frustration of trying to draw symmetrically. Next, I scan the drawing into Adobe Illustrator, which is a pretty simple program. I then re-render it nice and clean, make a copy of the rendering, flip the copy and connect it to the original to create a clean computer rendering of the full symmetrical design. If you have Adobe Photoshop on your computer, you most likely have Illustrator as well, so from my experience you don't need any fancy CAD rendering programs. Notice how the original hand drawing (along with white-out marks) on the right compares with the cleaned up illustration on the left, which includes the additional interior construction screw holes (the EDM can create all the screw holes as well). Once I finish the rendering, I export the drawing as a DXF file to my local machine shop so they can cut the parts.

and taken advantage of this technology to produce three versions of the design. I'm creating three exact copies profile-wise of the design, yet each dagger will have completely different materials, so in a sense they will still be one-of-a-kind works of art. The fun thing will be to see how both similar and truly different these pieces will be from each other in the end. My goal in creating these was to offer a more economical alternative to my more elaborate one-of-a-kind pieces. In addition to the use of technology, I've simplified some of the signature design features and construction techniques to keep the time/cost down. In total, I completed these three daggers in 285 hours, which yes, is a lot of time invested, but in reality just under 100 hours each. This might sound extreme, but it's pretty exciting to me because I'd normally spend that entire 285 hours on just ONE of my knives!

Design-wise I came up with a few new tricks as well, due to thinking of things in a new way. This has led to more possibilities and an entirely new approach in construction that would have otherwise not been possible without incorporating the use of some technology.

In particular, I've been dabbling in the use of EDM (Electro-Discharge Machine) for about three years now. I prefer EDM to laser or water-jet for it's perfect accuracy, cleaner finish, and ability to cut thick parts, while still retaining perfect 90-degree angle tolerances. This means you can stack and cut multiple parts at once, without losing any dimensional accuracy, as I did for this project. Even though I'm now utilizing this technology, I don't actually own an EDM myself, nor do I know any fancy computer programs. I still like to keep things as simple as possible. All I do is scan my drawings into my computer, then using Adobe Illustrator, vectorize my original drawings, then save and export them as a DXF file. The local machine shop takes it from there. As far as my use of EDM goes, for the most part all I'm really doing is saving a ton of band-saw and drill-press work; most everything else is still done with simple machines and by hand. The work you'll see on my website and here in the project is still mostly hand made.

# Safety

Before we begin, it's important to take a moment and remember safety equipment. EYE PROTECTION is always essential, and hearing protection, and a respirator are also things I suggest using for many common metalworking processes. Recently I took a big step towards taking better care of my health while in the shop, and purchased a $6000 industrial full shop dust collection system. It's been worth every penny; my shop is cleaner, which makes production way more efficient, I feel leaps and bounds better in terms of my overall health, and I don't come home to my wife at the end of the day caked in dirt!

Before starting work it's important to check and maintain the condition of your tools. They should be clean, organized and well oiled. Cutting equipment should be new and sharp, and work areas should be clean and roomy. Also, most important for the type of precision we are trying to achieve is that work surfaces are perfectly square with tool contacts such as band saw blades, grinding belts, and your drill press chuck. You also want to make sure that tooling directions are facing away from you, and that the distance (gap) between work tables and cutting/grinding tools is the tightest it can be without causing interference of normal machine operation.

# Materials

Both my website and facebook page have a lot of valuable resources that you might find useful, including links to photos of my studio fully illustrating my tools, and equipment, and descriptions of their use. My main website also has educational resources and info regarding different types of materials, a glossary of terminology, etc. NOT found openly on my website is a *backdoor* link to my list of materials suppliers: www.jensenknives.com/suppliers

The following is a list of materials that I used to create this particular project: Damascus steel, gold-lip pearl, abalone, fossil mastodon ivory, titanium, gold, gemstones, gold leaf.

# Tools/Machines

EDM
A large clean work bench
Dust collection system
Drill press
Milling machine
2" x 72" variable speed belt grinder/sanders
Precision granite plate
Jewelers bench
Ultrasonic cleaner
Engraving vice
1" x 30" belt sander
Heat-treating oven
Heat treating foil
Steel quenching blocks
Mini lathe
6" x 60" variable speed belt grinder/sander
Anodizing area and equipment
Etching area and equipment
Grinding clamp
"Scotch" brand 'permanent' double stick tape
Crazy glue
Square, small polishing buffs
Small hand saw
Jewelers files
Sharpie marker
Dykem
Measuring calipers
Small clamps
Scribe
Rawhide mallet
Stone-setting punches
Drill bits
Acetone
Q-Tips
Nail polish
Brownells baking lacquer
Gilding size
Number punch set
1-2-3 precision blocks
Hand tap wrench
2-56 taps
4-40 taps
2-56 screws
4-40 screws
Sand paper
Cutting burs
Split mandrels
Heavy duty wire cutters
Jewelers saw
Flex shaft
Small slotted screw driver

For this project, I actually made three of this design, and this is the first time I've ever done this. I've been exploring the use of EDM for a couple of years now, but to this point I've still only used it to make one-of-a-kinds, primarily using it for its ability to accurately cut any complicated shape I can dream of. Now, I really take advantage of this technology, as I cut out all the parts for three knives at once. I could stack even more together if I wanted to. Here, I laid out the design for the integral blade on three separate pieces/patterns of Damascus steel. I also came up with a new design feature which lets me have cross-guards while still using a relatively narrow piece of steel, and therefore not have a ton of scrap material. The cross-guards dovetail into the main body of the knives, additionally secured by hidden screws. Using EDM, I know the dovetailed pieces will be a perfect tight fit thanks to the precision of the EDM. When done, the blade and guard will pretty much look like one complete piece. The Cross-Guard pieces are towards the bottom of the steel billets. It took some time to figure out the best placement of the design so that there was symmetrical pattern consistency through all three daggers, and so all parts could be cut in one pass. I do the same process with the three sets of bolsters.

# Start

Because this work is so complicated, my first step is to always draw and refine everything on paper, working out all of the issues in terms of design, proportion, materials, etc. And of course in this instance to get my EDM work finished. In my opinion, there's too much time, money and effort involved in making knives to start anything without a complete understanding of everything involved. You should know exactly where you're going to end up before you start. Of course, sometimes design changes and new ideas come up along the way, and I encourage you to incorporate them if you can, but my finished product is generally a 98% match to the original drawing. I also don't let any particular material dictate any of the size or shape of my elements. So, it's important to have a lot of different materials on hand so I can create what I want, not what I'm limited to.

I'm really glad to be able to show you the complete construction of these knives, so lets get on with the show!

I lined up all the patterns and screwed the billets of Damascus together, so that everything could be cut in one pass. Scraps can be saved for use in other projects. With EDM, there is virtually no loss of material, only about 20 thousandths all around. The holes have been spotted as well. Because it's all computer aided, the accuracy is perfect, and all the holes through all parts line up exactly. Now all I have to do is thread them. The edge burn caused by EDM is not too bad either, and can be cleaned up with some 220 paper, then finished from there.

The advantage of EDM over other cutting methods is that no matter the thickness of material you are cutting, everything will remain perfectly square. Notice how the Cross Guards dovetail into the rest of the Blade. The precision of this is another advantage of EDM... making this by hand would never be as exact. The pieces fit so tight that I actually need a plastic mallet to lightly tap them into place.

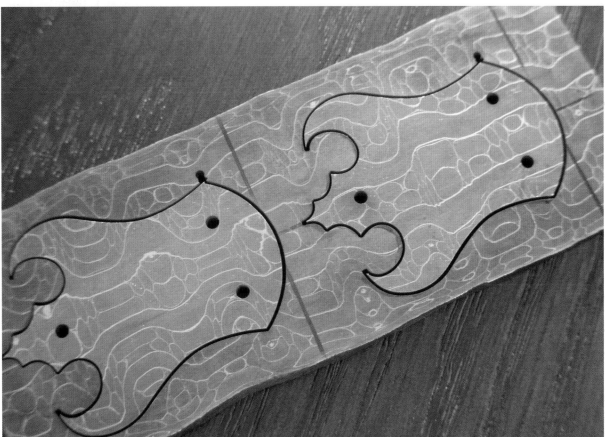

The bolster Damascus patterns are all completely different than the integral blade Damascus patterns. This set of bolsters has been placed in the now-negative space of the original material from which it was cut to illustrate the minimal loss of material.

In these 1/16" titanium pieces for the three different knives, holes are centered and placed perfectly and consistently through all parts.

Since EDM only cuts metal, and not natural materials, I can't use it to cut my handle materials, such as the pearl, abalone, and fossil ivory I used in these pieces. So, I had these additional steel templates made. Before going any further, I had to spend a good amount of time hand tapping (threading) over 125 holes for the three daggers.

Lining up handle material template onto some Gold-Lip Pearl, I used some double stick tape to initially hold them in place. I then drilled through all the holes in the template to transfer them into the pearl. Before doing so, I initially flat sanded all handle pieces on both sides to the same parallel thickness. This ensures all holes are square. Of course you want to first make sure that your drill press is perfectly square; I use a dial indicator set up in my drill chuck to help square things up. My drill press is accurate to within 1/2-a-thousandth of an inch.

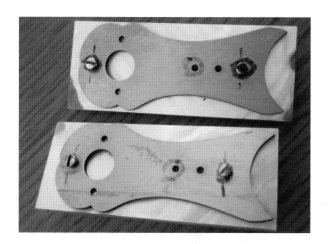

With the holes drilled, I threaded and screwed both the handle material and corresponding templates together, leaving them prepped to remove the excess material, which is done with a jewelers saw. The center detail hole is drilled/cut out. Cut just outside the edge of the template, leaving just a little bit of excess material. Later, the excess will be carefully ground back to the edges of the templates. All of this is repeated for the abalone, and fossil mastodon ivory handle materials. Before we get to that, let's address a few issues posed by the mastodon ivory scales.

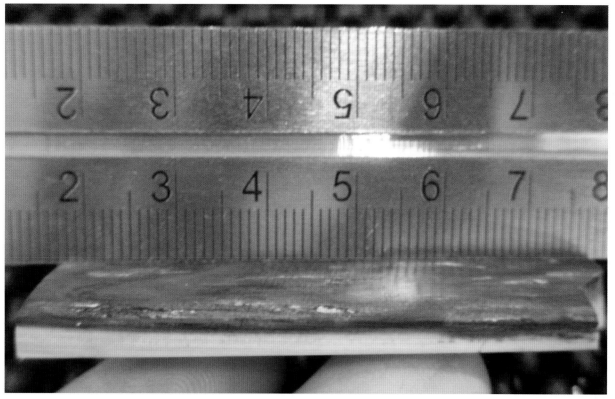

The fact that the outside of a mastodon tusk is inherently curved poses an issue that has to be dealt with. It's much easier to work with materials that are parallel. With mastodon ivory, the good color is at the surface and does not usually extend too deep, so we want to maintain as much of this color as possible. The problem with ivory is that it is also curved in two directions. The long direction is what needs to be evened out first. Luckily this pair of ivory had exceptionally deep color, so I roughly flat sanded the length on a belt sander using a fine grit belt and followed the short curve, which will help even things out. It's important to take extreme caution to not over-heat the ivory. It's also best to use ivory that has been rough-cut along time ago. This set of ivory had been stabilized in my materials collection for over 10 years, so it's well acclimated and remained pretty flat in storage over the years. A straight edge ruler shows the flatness achieved on the outside of the fossil mastodon scales after some initial sanding. I did this to both pieces and eyeballed that both of them, curvature-wise, were roughly the same. You can see how deep the color is even after some initial sanding. There's more sanding to do later to blend them into the bolsters, but I'm pretty confident I won't expose any of the white cores. I also flat sanded the bottoms, again making sure the rough curvature was even from side to side and centered in the middle.

This mark on the edge shows the actual thickness needed to match the thickness of the bolsters that the ivory will eventually be mated to. I'll remove the excess material from the backside so as not to lose any more of the color.

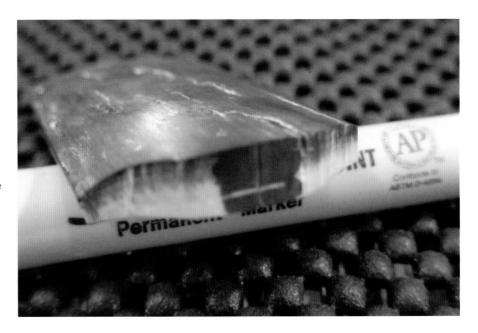

An ivory scale was set up in the mill, edge up, to make it square, taking care to not shrink the width past what I needed for the knife. Be careful to not crank the vice so tight as to damage the ivory.

After squaring up the edges, I put the scales in the milling vice upside down to remove the extra material from the backside. Milling enough of the side edges allows this to be set up firmly and squarely in the mill in order to evenly mill out some of the backside. I used a mill as opposed to just sanding the excess for two reasons: 1. There is a lot of material to remove and sanding would take too much time, and 2. Sanding would heat the material too much, causing other problems.

I removed material down close to the desired thickness with a few passes. From there, I slowly removed material from the center outward to even out the back side, stopping just short of hitting the sides of the vice with the mill and leaving a small flashing of material which can be filed off later.

With the scales at the desired thickness, I lightly flat sanded the backside of the ivory to remove milling marks. I marked out a centerline on the back and clamped the templates to the rear side. Drilling holes in fossil ivory is a challenge because of the innate curvature of the outside, so everything needs to be done from the backside.

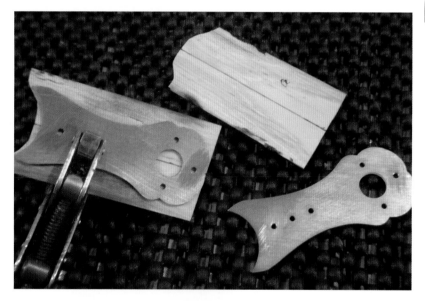

As part of set-up, after lining up the templates to the centerline on the bottoms, I clamped them and a steel ruler to the flat backside. The ruler acts as a "suspension bridge" for drilling. I also placed a few pieces of masking tape on the front so the drill bit wouldn't chip the face when it broke through.

The pair of precision 1-2-3 blocks supports the steel ruler. The ivory is clearly suspended off the table, but I know it's square to the table through both the previous milling processes and the use of the precision 1-2-3 block supports and ruler bridge. This also ensures that I know the holes that I drill from the backside are straight, centered and square. This is a great trick for drilling ivory.

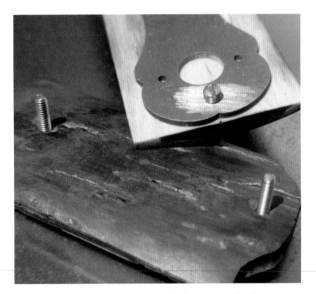

The drill holes are square and clean (no chipping) on the front thanks to the tape. Once the holes were in place in the ivory, I threaded them and screwed the templates into place. The clamps are no longer needed. I then used a jewelers' saw to rough-cut just outside the template, removing all the extra material.

Wrap the split mandrel with 600 grit sand paper and secure with masking tape. Split mandrels are very handy in doing finish edge sanding. I have many of these in different sizes to fit a variety of small curves. I use these in both the drill press and in a hand held flex-shaft. This is set up in the drill press to assure a perfect 90-degree square finished edge on the handle material. I used this to remove the small amount of extra material left when I initially cut the profile of the scales. I used a magic marker to darken the edges of the scales, which lets me know exactly where I'm working. The handle materials are all screwed down to templates, so when the black disappears as the side of the mandrel hits the steel template edge, I know I'm done. I go over each of the scales twice over to ensure a very fine finish. Also, as I work, the sand paper wears a bit, so in the end the finish is probably more of an 800-grit finish.

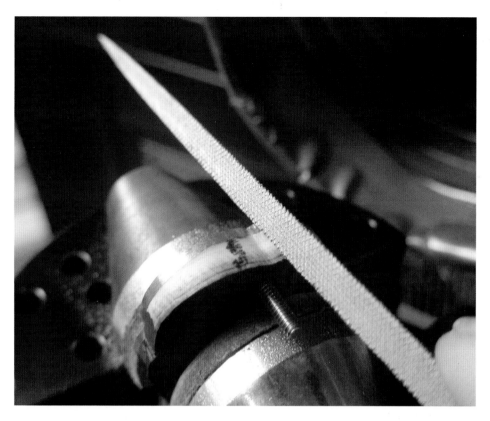

After finish profiling the edges of all three sets of handle materials, I removed the "V" shaped area that the round sanders couldn't quite get into with a small jewelers file. Next I finished the "V" grooves with 800 grit sand paper taped to a flat piece of steel, blending everything together. Once that was done, I finished everything off with a final buff and paste polishing.

After the 2nd round of edge sanding, I polished all of the edges of the scales using a small buff in a handheld flex-shaft. I polished the scales with the templates in place to ensure that I did not round over the bottom edge, so it's still nice and square. Rounding over of the top side edge doesn't matter because I'll still later be convex shaping the tops of the scales. Here, you can clearly see the finished rounded "V" grooves along the sides.

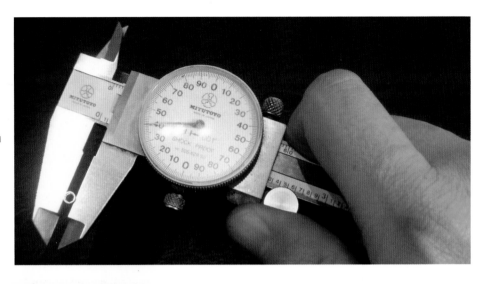

After figuring out the bezel width, I countersink the current screw holes in the bolsters and scales to a size just slightly under the width of the bezel.

This piece was held in the milling vice via folder pivots threaded onto the extra screw lengths, which saved the screw threads from getting mangled by the tension of the vice. Again, I know the holes in the handle scales are all lined up and centered because they were originally spotted by the EDM. After taking the same diameter sized drill bit that fit the current holes, I used them to line up the milling machine to each hole by making micro adjustments of the milling machine table and vice. Once I lined up the current small holes with the drill chuck, I countersink these holes to the right size opening through a two-step process: first with a mid size drill bit, bigger than the current hole but smaller than the final hole diameter, then with a target size drill bit. The two-step process is time consuming, but is better for softer materials, as removing less material per step is less harmful to the material: it keeps it cool, avoids chipping, deflection, shifting, etc. Repeat for all holes in all six handle scales.

The countersunk holes in the bolsters are just about a thousandth of an inch or so undersized to get a nice tight compression press fit for the bezels later. I'll also need to adjust the depth later.

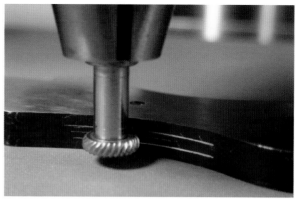

All the bolsters edges are now finished from 180 grit to 220, 320, 400, and finally to 600. This took a long time due to all of the hard to reach areas. I used different sized split mandrels in a flex shaft to do this. The bottom flats were finished out to 220, but I had not done anything to the top flats because I later convex-curve the top surface together with the handles material. The top surfaces will get finished after that.

At this point, an addition to the bolster edges being finished, the flat areas of all other metal parts had been sanded to a 600 grit finish and the rest of the edges to 220 grit. All parts had also been stamped 1-3 to correspond to which knife they were part of, and all front side parts are stamped #1, rear: #2. This way no parts get confused or out of place. The stamps were all on the back or on areas not visible in the finished pieces.

Taping down some 600 grit sand paper to the table of the drill press, I did some special carving along the edge of the blades. The 600-grit paper is the same as the current finish of the flats of the blades, so as I moved the pieces around the finish will stay the same. I used the drill press to do some side carving along the knife handle area. I placed a precision pivot bearing onto the shaft of the cutting tool since the shaft was so narrow; this widens the shaft, and thus becomes my cutting tool side-depth stop. I also set the height of the cutting tool in the drill press chuck, so that the concave grove I cut is centered. Once the machine was running, I moved the dagger into the sides of the cutting tool.

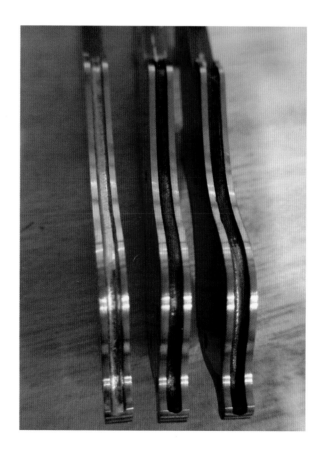

All finished. This process is a pain to do: side cutting into stainless Damascus really kills the cutting tool. It took about six hours per knife. It's slow and boring work, but creates a nice effect. You can see there is still some rough tooling marks, which need smoothing out. These grooves are all at an even depth due to the steel pivot depth stop. Just like finishing the handle scales, once the side of the pivot on the cutting tools wears off the Dykem on the original upper and lower edge, the cut is complete. After I finished, I cleaned up these side grooves to get rid of all the tooling marks with a small round diamond burr to even everything out.

To prep for what will become small milled flute details (blood-grooves in a sense, but shorter, so more decorative), I screwed one of the liners onto a blade, laid out some DyKem (the blue stuff), and scribed a center line from the liner tip and the blade tip. (I know both these reference points are perfectly centered because they were cut via EDM). Next, I figured out my top and bottom length and marked those as well.

On the backside, I screwed some large folder pivots onto the excess screw length (same as I did previously with the scales when I was opening up the countersinking). Again, these are what I end up clamping onto in the milling vise, and since the screw holes were spotted with the EDM, I know they are perfectly centered on the knife. Can you see why I'm a fan of technology? Getting this precise would be a total pain by hand and eye, and never as accurate.

The blade clamped into place via the pivot bolts on the screws. I know the blade is perfectly square to the mill, but I need to line up the cutting tool with the centerline. So, before milling I simply put a center point tool in a collet, and then micro adjusted the table forward and back until the tip lined up perfectly with the line. Then I switched out the center point tool with the actual cutting tool, in this case a 1/8-inch diameter ball end mill. After zeroing my height crank I went down 60 thousandths of an inch on both sides. The milling is pretty close to done.

Going back to the liners, I marked which holes needed to be countersunk in order to accommodate the internal construction screws. To get really good tight compression of parts, I reverse the screw direction, so that roughly ever other hole comes through from front, then back, front, then back, etc.

The internal construction screws will be eventually flush-set. These internal holes are threaded for a 4-40 screw for extra strength. Since these will never be seen in the final product you can use bigger, and therefore stronger screws. The heads still need to be turned down in the lathe, as they are a little too wide.

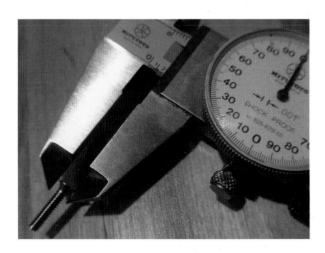

After measuring the width of the countersinks in the titanium liners, I measured the screw heads to determine how much needed turning down to fit the countersunk hole size in the liners. I needed to turn down 12 screws a little smaller than the countersunk holes in the titanium liners. Once the width was correct, I faced off the tops, as the screw heads were still too tall. Before that, I re-slotted the screws to a deeper depth so that, after trimming the fronts, I still had a usable slot. The screws were screwed into a folder pivot, then set in the lathe vise to avoid damaging the threads.

The screw width is good and the tops of the screws are fairly flush with the surface of the titanium.

After assembling the liners onto the blade frames, you can see how the layers create a stepped effect. From the front you'll see all of the different materials, patterns, and textures at once. You can also see the extra length of one of the screws. I painted the excess screw lengths with Dykem. Once it dried, I removed all the screws, cut the excess off with a jewelers saw, and de-burred and rounded off the ends so the threads wouldn't bind or catch on anything.

After cutting and grinding, I re-assembled everything, staggering the entry direction of the screws to ensure maximum compression of layers so everything is air- and light-tight. I colored the screw area to make sure nothing was too high. After a light flat sanding, I could tell that some of the screw heads and posts were still too high or too long. After checking every screw in this manner, I simply removed the extra length material in the lathe for the screw heads, or in the case of the posts just ground them off so that everything was slightly recessed below the flats of the liners. Internal construction screws were added through the liners and the dovetailed cross-guards to better secure them. The internal construction screws are threaded through all three parts.

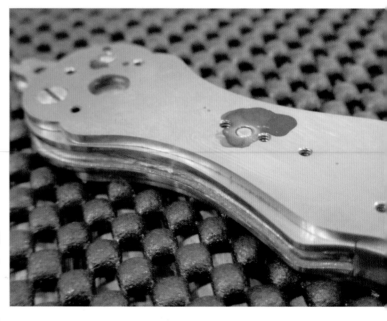

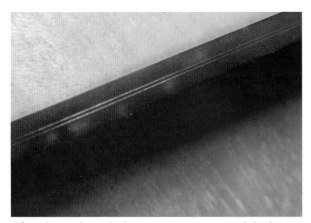

After doing the calculations (measure metal thickness, divide by two, then minus about 10-16), I scribed side grind lines along the edge of the steel in the blade area. The center area ended up about 20-26 thousandths of an inch.

In addition to the side edge grind scribe lines, I also scribed some face scribe lines to both sides of all three blades. These lines are 100 thousandths of an inch apart (a little less than an 1/8 inch). When grinding, by following one section at a time, the grinds come out evenly. I ground one or two line segments at a time on all four bevels before moving onto the next 100 thousandths of an inch section. Repeat for each section in that order.

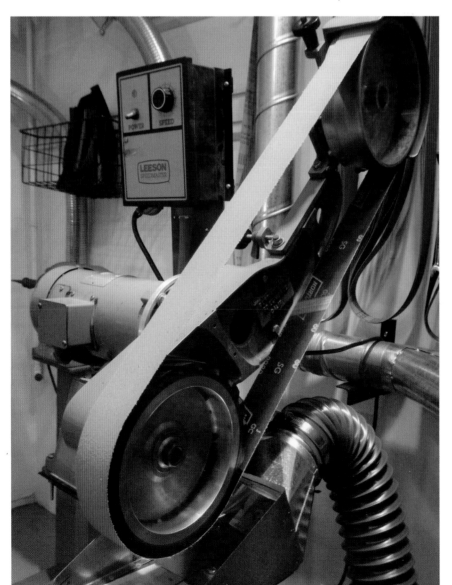

Using the variable speed "Burr King" blade grinder, I start out with a 60-grit belt to hog out the bulk of the material. Grinding the bevels is all done by hand on the machine, carefully sweeping and pushing the blade into and across a very small contact point on the wheel. Check out a video of me doing a little grinding on these at https://www. facebook.com/JensenKnives.

To start the bevel, I ground down to the side edge depth scribe lines, and into enough of the face depth to establish a slight concave groove. Start grinding before heat-treating, so that enough of the concave pocket is established to easily pick it up and fall back into it later. I kept the steel bulky to avoid warping during heat treating. As long as the start of the hollow grind is well established, the cutting wheel will fall back into the concave easily enough to finish the rest of the grind in the hardened state. Once hardened, it'll be harder and slower work, but I find that this resistance helps me work more precisely.

The prep bevels on all the blades, rough ground to the second scribe line, took about 15 minutes per bevel. I heat-treated the blades and finished the grinding one bevel at a time, one scribed section at a time, moving through a progression of finer grit belts.

Moving onto some file-work, the liner sets were screwed together and layout fluid applied along the front and side edges of the titanium liners. Layout lines were scribed 1/16 inch apart. I scribed depth lines along the fronts, also 1/16 inch deep, from the edge. Screwing liners together is a good little shortcut trick for file-work. From here I figured out what type of pattern I wanted, then made some start nicks in all the appropriate places to help avoid losing track and screwing up the repetitive pattern.

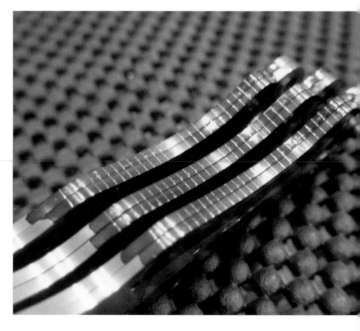

Using a small triangular diamond jewelers file, I made alternating carved "Vs". For this project I kept things pretty simple, but the pattern looks far more complicated when the liners are separated.

Once finished carving the pattern, I took the liners apart, sanded the flats to remove any burs, then screwed the liners back together. From there, I re-sanded the edges to a 600-grit finish to remove excess layout lines, and went back over the carvings with some 600-grit sand paper wrapped around the file.

Everything was once again taken apart, re-sanded to remove any burs, cleaned and desealed. Bolsters were screwed down to their corresponding liners.

On the backside of the assembly, you can see the excess screw lengths which need to be cut. In more complex pieces, I leave these because I thread the screws through all components. This makes for a better built knife but is a lot more time-consuming.

After placing Dykem around the cut screw nubs, I ground the screw nubs down just a little past the liner surface.

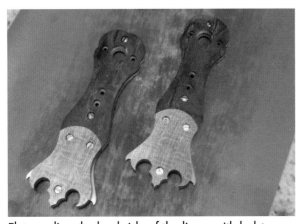

Flat sanding the backside of the liners with bolsters and scales in place, over some 600-grit sand paper placed on the precision granite plate, cleans up any burs.

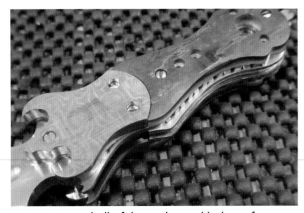

Next I removed all of the scales and bolsters from the liners and re-attached the liners with the internal construction screws back onto the main body of the blade, minus the cross-guards, (because they'd be in my way in the next process of handle contouring). I also re-attached the scales and bolsters.

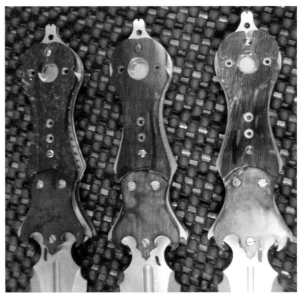

Coloring the handle surfaces of all three daggers helped me see where I was working when contouring the handles. I used Dykem for the steel areas, and a black Sharpie for the handle material. I prefer Dykem, but it tends to soak into material a bit, which is not good for porous materials such as the natural handle materials on these daggers. Instead I used the sharpie marker on the scales as the color stays on the surface. The coloring helps to make sure grinding is even from side to side and from top to bottom.

Round the handles using my large 6x60-inch variable speed belt grinder/sander, starting with a 320-grit belt. Handle contouring, or putting a convex surface on them, is done by rocking the handles side-to-side on the moving belt in an arcing motion. This is done very carefully and all by hand and eye coordination, making sure to check your progress often. By looking to see where the color is wearing, keep adjusting pressure to assure everything comes out evenly.

After making a little progress, I need to bring down the widest point the most – the flairs in the bolsters. There is a lot of pressure adjusting happening all the time. In addition, make sure the handle heights are equal from front to back, and the curvature is equal from side-to-side. Since the ivory already has a natural curve to it, I needed to bring down the sides of the bolsters to match the ivory first, then blend everything together from there.

Looking low and up from the tip of the blade, you can clearly see the curvature of the handle. In this case I was also being careful to not over-do it and nick the small side protruding tips of the titanium liners. If those tips were not there I could have curved the handles a little more. This is another reason the cross-guards as inlays work out so well, as they would pose problems during this process if not removable. If the cross-guards were integral, I'd have to do this process without assembling the full knife, and by only holding onto the liners and their corresponding handle materials and curve from there. That works as well, but there is a lot less to hold onto. After finishing all the handle shaping to 400-grit, I re-marked everything with Dykem and Sharpie, then re-sanded to 600-grit, repeating to finish at 800-grit.

After the handle contouring was all finished, I took everything apart, cleaned and de-burred once again. After rounding the handles, I had to re-countersink some of the holes, especially out towards the edges that got a little shallow in depth due to the shaping. I also placed some temporary screws in the holes that are not construction screw holes. These extra holes will later have set stones in them, as will the holes with screws. I placed screws in all of the holes so, when I polish the handles, the hole edges will not get rounded over. This is not a concern for the steel, but the natural handle materials are soft, so the holes could get a little rounded over from polishing. The screw heads prevent this from happening. Here, the scales and bolsters are all polished. I achieved this by placing the handles in the rotating vise by clamping onto the excess screw lengths coming out the backside. I then used the flex shaft with a small polishing buff to carefully polish the surfaces, using both hands for control. I also set my dust collection hose right up to the work area to suck away all of the nasty stuff while polishing. I first ran the buff against the "grain" of the sanding marks, then reverse from that. The trick is to run the buff pretty fast, with light pressure, and to keep it moving... you have to be very careful polishing natural handle materials as they can actually gouge in places if you don't keep the buff moving. Also, you have to be careful of rounding over the profile edges too much; you want to soften the edges a bit, but not change the overall profile. I spent about 20 minutes polishing each handle side. In the bolster steel, you can see the reflection of my hands holding the camera, which gives an indication of how well polished these are.

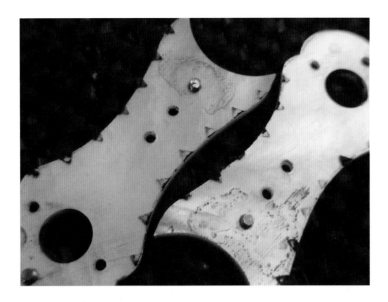

The remnants of the polishing compound are visible along the edges on the underside of the pearl handles. This dirt ended up in the recesses of the file work from the titanium liners, which are pretty large. When holding the finished knife in the right direction, you will be able to see these little triangular sections of the underside of the scales, so I needed to make sure these underside edges were finished and polished as well. This is the type of attention to detail that really takes your work to the next level.

Since every type of steel has different heat-treating instructions, I'm going to leave out instruction on heat-treating. You'll need to base this on whatever type of steel you're using in your own creations. I will say that I like using heat-treat foil, and air quenching steel between two thick blocks of steel. I've found this process keeps things clean, and the steel blocks remove any possible warping and cools fast.

After heat-treating, all parts were cleaned of any scale and taken back to 800 grit. The blades were placed in a grinding clamp, making sure the shoulders of the blades were square to the ends of the clamp. The grinding clamps ensure a nice, even straight line across the fronts of the blades as the hollow grinds are moved inward.

As the grinds move towards the center, you can see the Damascus pattern revealed. The majority of metal removal is done on a serrated contact wheel using an 80-grit belt, again following the rule of moving in one scribe line, one bevel at a time. Once the bulk of the work was done, I switched to a non-serrated wheel and dialed the speed control down to about 1/4 full speed.

The grinds finished to 320-grit. Ultimately I took the blades to an 800-grit finish, polish, then acid etch. I applied some Dykem to the blades so that when I went to the next grit (400) I could clearly see where I worked. Repeat this process for both 600 and 800-grits. Here you can clearly see where the sanding belt is hitting. The bluing shows where I worked and ensured I hit all spots, so that there were no old scratches left behind. The centerline sort of happens by itself, but also takes a lot of finesse to get perfectly straight. It took about an hour to finish through each consecutive grit (400, 600, 800) for the three blades.

All three daggers were finished to an 800-grit paper polish.

After finish-sanding and polishing every surface of the cross guards and bolsters, I masked off the areas that I did not want etched with several coats of nail polish. This included the area of the cross guards where they fit precisely into the blades, as well as the bottoms of the bolsters, all screw holes, and the rear edge of the bolsters where they fit up against the handle scales. It's important to do this to keep the tight, flat fits between parts, as well as the threaded screw holes. If not, these areas will etch out and change the dimensions making screws loose and contact areas no longer airtight. Let the nail polish dry fully overnight before proceeding with etching. You can also see that I left the underside tips of the bolsters un-masked; those do need to be etched as part of the final design as they will be seen. Any excess nail polish is cleaned up with acetone-soaked Q-Tips. After additional cleaning, de-greasing, etc., all parts are now ready for etching.

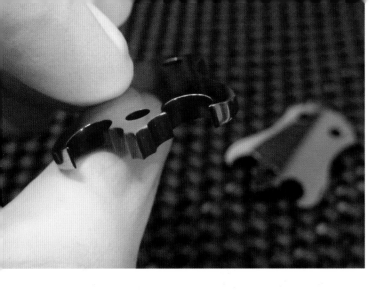

On this pair particular set of bolsters, I also masked off the polished front edges. Using multiple surface treatments creates some visual interest. These front areas will be nicer remaining mirror polished, rather than etched, since these particular patterns are incised straight-layer Damascus patterns, which means pattern-wise they are not very interesting once etched along the edges, unlike a mosaic or twist pattern.

For the cross guards, in addition to the areas masked off for mechanical reasons, I also masked off some areas for design effect, as with the bolsters. Again, these inside curls will look cooler with a mirror finish rather than etched.

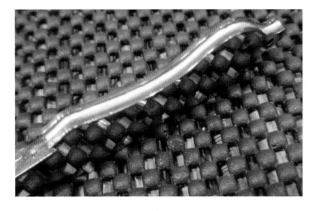

On one of the knives, I also decided to mask off the side rails on either side of the concave edge carving. This made those side groves really pop.

The large tub of etching solution is a 50/50 mix of ferric chloride and distilled water. Everything is handled in the etching process using latex gloves. Some steels call for different etching mixtures and times, so check with your supplier. In the three part neutralizing set up, after etching the pieces first go into TSP (tri-sodium phosphate), then baking soda, and finally Windex. A good 10-minute soak in each does the trick. While etching, materials are constantly scrubbed with a soft toothbrush to remove disintegrating metal from low spots, and high spots are lightly sanded in the solution with 1000 grit paper.

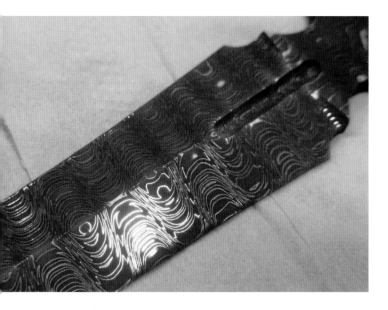

Once in the etching solution, the pattern becomes visible. You can get a nice even surface in about five minutes if everything is really clean. I like to etch a little longer to create topography between the high and low areas of the pattern to really bring them out. I usually etch until I can feel the ridges defining the two materials with my fingernail. Here is one of the blades after a 10-minute etches. The bright silver lines are the result of all the fine finishing work these three daggers went through, creating some really nice contrast. At this point the nail polish still needs to be removed, and in this case the blade needed to be re-buffed because I planned to hot-blue this one.

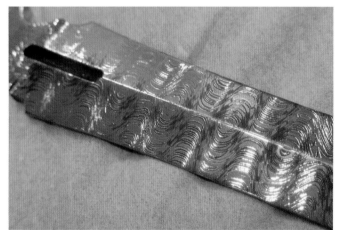

After a full polishing in preparation for hot-bluing, I sent this to a friend to do the bluing. After polishing, I cleaned and degreased the blade again.

Notice the detail of the finish etching on one of the other blades.

After seeing the edge of the dagger done with the side rail masking on, I wished I'd done this to the other two daggers.

After bluing, in addition to the overall blue color, there are some nice purple highlights. There's an amazing amount of chatoyancy, which is an optical illusion of depth and movement created by the combination of Damascus pattern, finishing, deep etching and bluing. You can also see the difference in finish in the milled groove detail, which was not finished to a mirror finish, so is much darker and more matte, creating a nice contrast and helping it to stand out against the flashy surrounding areas.

At this point, the top set of bolsters looks a little weird because I really deep etched them (for about 45 minutes). I did this on purpose, as a deep etch is required for the last finishing technique I did on this particular set. The second set has been etched, buffed, hot-blued and is now done. The bottom set has been etched and finished naturally.

The deep-etched set was coated with about 10 coats of slowly built-up layers of Brownells Baking Lacquer. After letting everything dry really well between coats, I used acetone to clean up areas that I didn't want blackened, such as the high polished front edges, most of the bottoms, and the rear edge that meets the handle material. I also planned to use this stuff selectively in the hollow grinds of one of the blades.

I also had to apply the baking lacquer to the small areas on the underside that will be seen in the finished piece.

The deeply-etched blade, with baking lacquer applied, is ready to bake. In preparation for this, I had not previously fully tempered this blade and the bolsters after heat-treating because I knew I was going to heat them again for the baking lacquer process. The blade and bolsters were baked for a half hour at 300 degrees F. Next, all excess overspray was carefully sanded off the high spots, leaving the lacquer in the deep etched recesses only. I finished by polishing the lacquer, which takes a really nice high gloss shine.

After baking the lacquered parts, I set up one of the lacquered bolsters in a leather-faced vice via some screws protruding from the rear. Using the sanding block, I carefully flat-sanded the high spots of the bolsters, following the curvature. WARNING: LEAD POISON HAZARD! The baked lacquer dust contains lead. Wear a dust mask and crank your dust collection system or vacuum. Also be careful to not over-sand; just hit the high spots of the Damascus bringing them back to bare metal, and keeping the low spots filled with the lacquer. This is why I deep etched the blade and bolsters so much, to make sure that there is about 10 thousandths of an inch of lacquer covering the low spots. Sand just enough of the lacquer in the recesses so that the finish is even and they will polish up perfectly.

Sanding finished, tops exposed so the pattern is once again fully visible, and ready to polish.

Desk Daggers: A Limited Edition Jensen Knives Trio

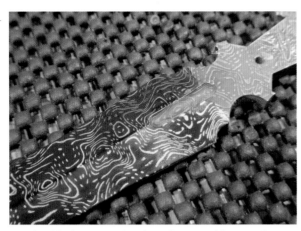

For the blade, I went back to the variable speed blade grinding machine and set the belt speed to a slow crawl, using an 800 grit sanding belt to carefully re-sand the tops just like I did with the bolsters. The high spots of the blade grinds were now exposed and polished. You can really see the intended contrast here between the now-glossy black blade grinds and the more industrial grey looking blade, milled groove and ricasso.

I applied some layout fluid along the edges of all three blades. I then scribed a light line with my calipers along the edge, 40 thousandths of an inch high, in preparation for sharpening. I prefer a finished edge geometry of around 32 degrees, which I achieve given the current edge thickness of roughly 20 thousandths of an inch and this newly scribed face height of 40 thousandths of an inch.

I set up my Burr King belt sander so the belt was at the edge target geometry angle of 32. Following the lightly-scribed guide line, I used the slack part of the belt to sharpen with a low-medium speed. With the belt running, I swept the blade edge across the belt, holding the blade parallel to the floor.

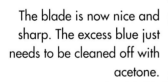

The blade is now nice and sharp. The excess blue just needs to be cleaned off with acetone.

Blade's Guide to Making Knives

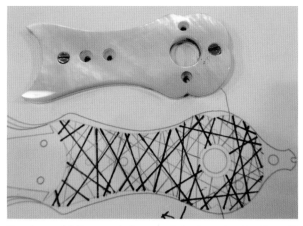

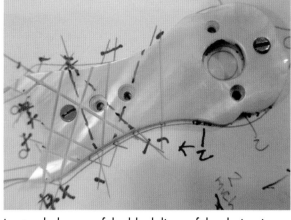

For the gold-lip pearl dagger, I designed a "rutilated" carved effect for the scales. You can see the sketch pencil lines under the black lines that I finally settled on as my design; this took some work to get the right proportions.

I extended some of the black lines of the design in pencil so I could lay the pearl on top, see the design underneath, and transfer it to the pearl. You can see the start of some of the incising of the pearl, which was done with a jeweler's saw.

The gold-lip pearl scales were finished and coated twice over with 22k dark lemon yellow gold leaf. This process starts by applying a coat of gilding size with a brush, trying especially to get it into the cut crevices. Once the pieces are well saturated, you wait about an hour and a half to let the size get to the proper tackiness. Then, using another brush, you pick up small pieces of the leaf and jab it into place, in this case trying to get into the crevices. Due to the nature of this design, most of the gold leaf was wasted on the top surfaces. The excess was later carefully removed by gently rubbing.

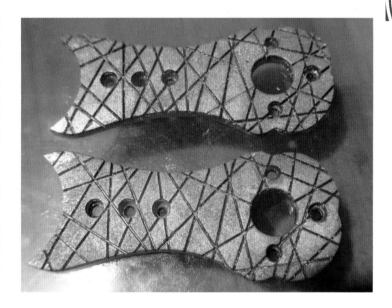

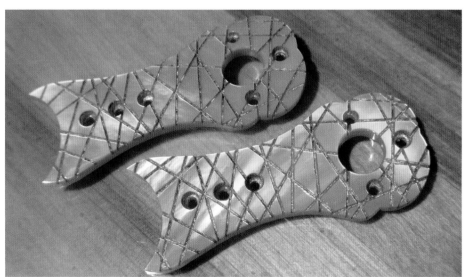

All excess leaf was removed from the top surfaces to reveal the gold-lip pearl again, so it's now finished. It's not a lot of contrast, but it makes the lines pop a little.

A finished pair of anodized liners was placed on the blue blade. To help with anodizing, I have a color chart which corresponds to every number on the rectifier dial, which tells my what color I'll get at each number. For example, if I want blue shade #20, I just dial that in on the rectifier. The anodizing set up and process is pretty simple: distilled water and tri-sodium phosphate are mixed in a small plastic food container, and a large piece of submersed anodizing foil is attached to the black lead of the rectifier. The work-piece to get colored is connected to a red lead wire, the rectifier gets turned on and the piece is dipped into the bath, and color appears pretty much instantaneously.

Part of finishing these knives is completing the stone setting. This 18k gold bezel was measured with calipers, this time for height. I wanted to make sure I had 65 thousandths of an inch of bezel recessed into the handles; this would anchor the settings well into the handle materials, yet leave just enough proportion of gold and of course the set stone slightly raised above the surface of the handle.

After going back and measuring the depth of all holes using the depth-measuring end of the calipers, I made some adjustments. I then shaved off the tops of these screws in the lathe so that everything ended up at the desired depth of 65 thousandths of an inch. In the case of the couple holes for the set stones that don't have any screws in them, I simply re-countersank them to the correct depth.

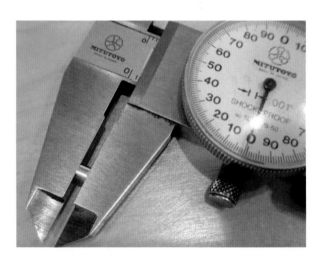

Next up is stone setting, so I needed to figure out which stones to use on each knife. I placed a bunch of different types of stones in bezels and then moved them all around my work. By process of elimination, I narrowed down which stones went best with each dagger.

I carefully hand polished all of the now bezel-set stones on the small flex-shaft buff with the hand-piece set in a bench top holder and speed controlled with a foot pedal. For this process, it helps to have longer fingernails to hold those small pieces. After polishing, everything was ultrasonically cleaned, rinsed and the undersides especially blown out with compressed air. From there it was time to start final assembly. First, I took everything apart using latex gloves and gave everything a final cleaning with a deerskin shammy before re-assembling. Final assembly started with sliding the dovetailed cross guards into place, then screwing down the liners to full compression and applying a small drop of glue to the threads before inserting them. Next came the bolsters, again using a small drop of glue on the screw threads, then finally the same with the handle scales.

Now ready to set some stones, you can see the angled, concave cone shape of the underside of the setting punch. The bezels I used were perfectly calibrated, solid gold with no solder seams, of uniform height and with a machined step on the inside for the stone to rest on. The stones were all machine cut, perfectly calibrated and color matched, natural gemstones from Austria. Twelve 2.5mm set stones and 42 3mm set stones went into the three daggers. All the gold was 18k royal yellow at a total weight of just over .3 ounces. The stone setting punch works by placing the stone in the bezel, then placing the punch squarely over the rim of the bezel. You then simply give the top of the stone setting punch handle a few light whacks with a rawhide mallet. I usually give it one good whack, then visually check to see if enough metal has folded over the top edge of the stone, and make sure the stone is still centered on its bezel seat. Then I usually give it another two light whacks for good measure, making sure to not overdo it or you risk cracking the stone. To make sure the stones are really secure, I take the bezel set stone and drop the assembly onto a wood table from a height of about six inches or so. If the stone doesn't fall out from that, you know your setting is good.

# In conclusion

Thank you for following along on this little journey. I did want to take this time to address a couple of points:

I am in no way, nor have I ever been, caught up in the hand-made vs. machine-made debate. My philosophy is to make the best, and coolest damn knives I can, and frankly I think my own knives have become considerably cooler since incorporating some of the modern technology that I've just shared with you. However, I do firmly believe that knowing how to make things by hand is not only an honorable pursuit, but also instills and refines ones own precision, innovation, problem solving,

and countless other skill sets. I see no reason not to use technology, it's just another tool. It's also important to be honest with both yourself and your clients as to your true abilities. Technology provides no greater satisfaction than knowing how to make something with your own two hands. There is no substitute for the type of education, knowledge, and understanding that simple, repeated practice contributes to your work. I'm here today, given this forum to share and speak to you, because I'm a master of my craft, which came about only through hard work and practice.

I believe in sharing, openness and honesty, and

All that was left to do was the friction fitting of all the stones. If everything went right, the set stones would be attached to the knives via a nice tight press fit only; a perfect fit is when I can press the set stone assembly part way into the holes just using my fingers. Then to fully set them down to the bottom of the hole, I use a rawhide mallet to tap the rest of the stone down. If the stone seems too tight to press fit, it's important not to force it. The best thing to do is to re-polish the bezel sides, which removes a few microns of gold and should be enough to get to the proper fit. In this photo, you can see one stone on the right all finished, with just a nice little rim of gold still present, which results from the proper countersink depth. Most of the gold is tightly recessed into the knives which ensures that they won't come out, yet there is still enough of the tops popping out that you get to see some of the gold. This also adds extra dimension to the handles. It takes a lot of work to get these proportions right. The bezel/stone assembly on the left is centered over the hole, ever so slightly press-fit in place, and ready to be fully set.

To protect the stone and other surfaces, I placed a thick piece of deer-skin shammy over the finger press-fit stone assembly. Then, using the rawhide mallet I gently tapped the top of the stone so it slid straight down and hit bottom. If any bezel ends up being a bit loose, you can scuff up a little bit of the bottom half of the outside of the bezel with a file, apply a tiny drop of crazy glue to the outsides, then proceed with the press fit once again. It's important to make sure not to get any glue on the bottom of the bezel, as the glue fumes can create a minor coating on the back side of the stone and cloud the color. Also, a little extra glue may come up to the surface, so make sure to hit the surface area just around the set stone with a little acetone on a Q-Tip.

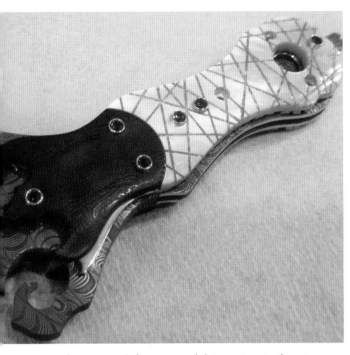

A few stones left to set and this project is done!

in that spirit I ask all that view my words and photos, or learn and incorporate from my knowledge base or anyone else's, that you give credit where credit is due. I, and the rest of the makers in this book, have worked long and hard to share our knowledge. Together the experts in this book are helping you shave off countless years of trial and error, and it's only fair to acknowledge us. I truly hope that you've learned a lot, and will continue to pass knowledge along, so that this vibrant community continues to grow.

Thank You.

In parting, I invite you to check out my website (http://www.jensenknives.com), and stop by my facebook page to say hello sometime (https://www.facebook.com/JensenKnives ).

Sincerely,

*John Lewis Jensen*

# Making the Using Knife

## by Tim Zowada

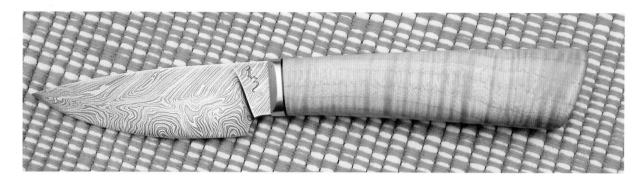

When discussing the making of a using knife, the first thing to decide is – what in the world is a "using" knife? Okay. It is obviously a knife that is meant to be used. It is not primarily a showpiece or collectible. Although, it could be both of those, as long as the knife was still useful as a tool. As we begin the process of "making the using knife" we need to decide how the knife will be used and what the thing will look like.

A using knife will be able to perform the tasks for which it is intended. That may sound like a pretty obvious statement, but there is really a lot to it. We need to figure out what the knife will be used for, most of the time. Knives are used for a lot of things. Will the primary use be hunting, combat, diving, kitchen use, whittling, or just pealing apples? The primary use of the knife will determine not only its shape and size, but also give direction to the steel choice, edge geometry, handle material, heat treatment and a number of other details.

Very few people these days carry knives on a daily basis. Of those that do, most rarely use it. A good using knife will practically beckon the owner to put it on and take it everywhere, compelling them to look for things to cut.

## Design

The using knife for this chapter will be a knife that an average person could use on a daily basis for most routine cutting chores. Even so, it will be great at some things, and lousy at others. It could be used as a weapon, but a gun would be better. It could also be used to slice cucumbers, but a dedicated chef's knife would be better there as well. This will be a knife that will be right at home, and even excel, at things like at cutting apples, string or paper, opening envelopes, stripping wire, trimming auto vacuum lines, cleaning brook trout, and even field dressing and skinning a deer, among other things. It will be a knife most of us would find useful, on a daily basis, for the majority of our cutting chores outside the kitchen.

## Size

The place to begin is the size and profile of the blade. If this knife is to be used often, you will want to have it with you all of the time. If the blade is too big, you will leave it at home. If it is too small it won't be able to handle some of the tougher jobs. A good compromise is to think, "what would I be willing to wear every day to the office, or even to church?" The largest blade that fits that concept will be a good size to carry on a daily basis. If you are afraid of getting the "stink-eye" from someone, the knife will either be concealed or left at home. Neither is very practical for a knife you want to carry and use frequently.

Concerning blade size, additional consideration must be given to local laws and statutes. Most state and local governments have limits on the maximum blade length allowed within their jurisdiction. Sometimes, these statutes will vary depending on whether the knife is fixed or folding, and if it is carried concealed or in the open. In most areas of the country this is in the 3-1/2 to four inch range for a fixed blade knife. It's kind of funny how these laws work. Where I live, I can carry a .44 Magnum revolver, concealed or out in the open, but I can't carry a four-inch folding pocket knife. Go figure! Be sure to check with local authorities.

A folding knife is also a good option for a using knife. Blade length limits apply here as well. A folding knife is a good idea if you prefer to carry the knife in your pocket or don't want anything on your belt. Folding knives won't be considered here as they are beyond the scope of this article. But, for a practical using knife, they are well worth considering.

## Blade shape and thickness

The discussion of various blade shapes tends to bring out strong opinions in the magazines and on the internet. The thing to remember is, the knife we are discussing is a compromise. The knife will be called on to do a little of everything. Taking another look at the partial task list above, and consider how the knife is actually held and used, it becomes aparent that a more "pointy" blade shape would be the most useful. The only area where the pointy shape would seem to be a hindrance would be for animal skinning. A pointy blade still works fine there, as long as the animal is skinned while warm, as it should be. A gentle curve along the entire edge will make slicing and pealing more efficient. A good friend calls this shape a "willow leaf" blade. That pretty much describes it.

Blade thickness is important to think about. A thinner blade will cut with less effort than one that is thicker. Remembering that the primary purpose of a knife is to cut stuff, it is desireable to keep the blade as thin as possible. Yet, the blade needs to be thick and strong enough to survive moderate abuse. This knife would be expected to cut through the pelvic bone of a deer, so the blade can't be too

thin or delicate. As with most things in life, a compromise will be reached between ease of cutting and sharpening versus strength.

Most knives are far too thick. This includes both factory and custom knives. There seems to be a prevalent concept in the knife community that a knife should also be useful as a pry bar. Remember, this tool is first, and most importantly, for cutting things. Start looking around. You will see that a really well made nine-inch chef's knife is about 3/32 inch thick at the handle, or about 0.93 inches. This is for a two-inch wide blade. Properly heat treated, those chef's knives will cut just about everything. The edge might be a little delicate for some tasks outside the kitchen, but not many. Our knife will be beefed up a little to be able to handle some of the rougher tasks.

Let's take a look at cross section geometry. The way these chef's knives are ground, the blade has about a 2-1/2° included angle in the grinding of the blade bevels. This is for the entire bevel, not the final sharpening angle. If we were to translate this to our 1-1/8 inch blade, we would have a blade thickness of 0.055" at the spine. A lot of small knives out there have spines of 3/16 (0.187) inch or even thicker. The thing to keep in mind is that thinner knives will cut better and easier. The more acute angles, along with less mass, simply cut through stuff with less effort. Thicker blades are stronger, but don't cut as well. Make the knife as thin as possible, as long as it will stand up to what you would consider moderate abuse.

Blade thickness is not just a consideration at the spine of the knife. How thin the edge is ground, before sharpening is very important as well. An extreme example would be to have a knife that is 0.090 inch thick at the spine and 0.030 inch thick at the edge. The knife would have a very shallow angle between the two sides, but be a lousy tool as the sharpening bevel would be well on its way to 90 degrees. The knife would be very difficult to sharpen, as there would be a lot of metal to remove. Re-sharpening a knife like this would be a nightmare. On top of this, the knife wouldn't cut well, as the blade would be very thick right behind the sharpening bevel. Unfortunately there are a lot of knives like this.

The best edge thickness, after grinding, will vary some depending on how severely the edge will be abused in normal use. Once again, thicker is stronger, thinner cuts better. A straight razor is usually ground to 0.001 inches thick at the edge, or less. Chef's knives, for delicate use, will be about 0.005 inch thick, after final grinding. For a small general use knife, 0.010 to 0.015 inch is a good thickness to shoot for.

The discussion of ideal spine and edge thickness is interesting and could go on for several pages. As the study of blade geometry goes "off the deep end," you will notice that different steel types as well as variations in heat treating will effect how thin the blade spine, and edge, can be. Steel composition choices and heat treatment options greatly influence the strength and abrasion resistance of the blade. If the chosen steel is "weaker" than it could be, the knife geometry will have to be beefed up to compensate.

## Steel choices

Today there are a number of excellent steels available. They all have their advantages and disadvantages. If this is a knife that will spend the majority of its time in a corrosive environment, a stainless steel would be the obvious choice. If edge retention and impact strength are the prime considerations, a good carbon steel would be a direction to consider. Fortunately for me, this article is about what I prefer and do. I make my own Tamahagane and pattern welded Damascus steel. The Damascus is a laminate of O1 and L6 tool steel. It is strong, holds an edge well, and is well suited for salt bath heat treating. So that is what will be used in this chapter.

Some decry the use of a non-stainless steel in a using knife. The claim is that it will quickly rust and become useless. The best response to this came from the late Jim Schmidt. He said, "A $30,000 Purdy shotgun will rust too, if it's not cared for properly. Things of value require some maintenance. Maintaining your treasures is part of the joy of owning them."

Damascus steel isn't at all a bad choice for a using knife. It is actually a great compromise. The etched surface is very easy to maintain and keep looking new. Maintenance is simple and easy, as long as the blade hasn't been allowed to rust. Properly welded and heat treated, high carbon Damascus holds a very good edge and is easy to sharpen. Of course Damascus steel is beautiful to look at as well.

## Handle

The handle on a using knife should be simple and "ergonomic." A knife is held in different ways for various tasks. If the handle were built so it only fit the hand in a hammer grip, it may not be comfortable or easily controlled when used with other grips. It must have a shape that works well in all the positions the knife will be used. The handle should not have any sharp corners or facets. They only hurt your hand. The only thing that should be sharp on a knife is the cutting edge of the blade.

A lot of consideration usually goes into the shape and size of the guard. This knife won't have one. A blade guard is useful on some knives, especially those where ones grip may slip during heavy use. On other knives, a guard simply gets in the way. A common task for an every day knife is cutting things on a board. This might be an apple, a carrot or even a piece of radiator hose. If there is a guard that drops below the edge of the blade, the knife becomes cumbersome to use.

The two basic types of handle construction are full tang and hidden tang. The full tang construction is where the tang also forms the profile of the handle. The handle material is then screwed or pinned to either side of the tang. Hidden tang construction is where the handle material completely surrounds the blade tang. Both constructions have their advantages. Hidden tang knives are lighter than their full tang counterparts. For a daily carry knife, weight is important. Hidden tang knives also have fewer and shorter joints, seams, and glue lines exposed to the elements. Our knife will use hidden tang construction.

Okay, it's finally time to get working on the knife. Now, this chapter isn't about how to make a simple or inexpensive knife. This is about how to make a high quality using knife. That means using the best materials and processes available to make the best tool possible. There are far simpler, and less expensive ways to make a good, useful knife. But, if the goal is to make the best knife possible, it is paramount to employ the best materials and techniques available.

Before starting, it is very important to emphasize the use of safety equipment during all stages of construction. An accident or moment of carelessness can change your life forever. Hand, ear, eye and lung protection should all be worn during the appropriate phases of construction. Don't underestimate the danger of wood and steel dust. The effects can add up over time. A dust mask or respirator will help save your lungs. Even with the high price, a 3M Airstream AS-400 helmet is a wise investment.

# Blade forging, for me

The primary reason to forge blades is that forging is simply more enjoyable than grinding. Forging also allows you to conserve material and make shapes and tapers that would be difficult and time consuming if only grinding or machining. That is not to say that forging is a significantly better way of doing things. It is just an option that many prefer.

Forging a blade is, very simply, taking a piece of steel, heating it and then hammering on it until it looks like a knife. It is really not much more complicated than that. There are, however, several details that should be considered.

Blades should only be forged within the correct temperature range for the type of steel being used. The manufacturers of tool steels publish recommended forging ranges for their steels. There are a lot of metallurgical reasons for the stated forging ranges, and it would take an entire article just to explain them. Simply stated, the internal structure if the steel will be far better off if you follow the manufactures recommendations. The blade will ultimately be stronger and stay sharper if temperature guidelines are followed closely.

The recommended forging range for this Damascus is 1550F to 1900F. This comes from combining the temperature specifications given for the O1 and L6 tool steels from which the Damascus is made. The actual forging temperature

Forging the Damascus stock to size on the 600lb steam hammer. The bar in author's left hand is a "stop block" to keep from forging the stock too thin.

The first step in forging the blade is to forge a point and taper the thickness of the bar stock.

can be determined with a pyrometer in the forge or, with practice, by eye. At the upper forging temperature, the blade is a medium to bright orange color in a dimly lit room. As the blade cools below the lower forging temperature limit, a phase transformation begins that is shown by shadows appearing on the blade surface. When the shadows appear, stop forging and reheat the blade. The shadows actually appear slightly below the lower forging limit. With practice, forging ends just before the shadows appear.

Forge atmosphere control is also a consideration. Various steels will react differently to *oxidizing* or *reducing* forge atmospheres. An *oxidizing* atmosphere is one where there is excess oxygen as compared to the amount of fuel (propane) being burned. A *reducing* atmosphere has an excess of fuel compared to the amount of oxygen available for combustion. The steels in this Damascus, O1 and L6, will lose carbon in a neutral to reducing atmosphere. They will lose iron, in the form of scale (iron oxide), but retain carbon, in a slightly oxidizing atmosphere.

Carbon is the element that allows the steel to harden. It is desirable to keep as much carbon in the steel as possible. For this reason, the forge should be set to have a slightly oxidizing atmosphere. Due to the possibility of decarburization and the usual pitting, the blade is forged about 0.015 inches oversize in all dimensions.

Begin forging by heating the blade to approximately 1850F. The blade is pulled from the forge

and the hammering begins. First, forge the blade tip profile and taper the thickness. This is usually best done at the same time. As the tip profile is forged, the blade will tend to squish out to the sides and get thicker. By alternately hammering on the edge and flat of the blade stock, the tip is shaped and the thickness controlled at the same time.

After the tip is profiled, the bevels are forged. By working with glancing hammer blows near the anvils edge, the edge is thinned to a thickness of about 0.030 inches. Start at the tip of the blade and work back to the tang area. Pay careful attention to forge the blade equally on both sides. Most smiths will usually heat the blade, hammer the bevel on one side, then reheat and do the other side.

After the blade profile and bevels are forged it is time to forge the tang. Cut the blade off of the bar and hold it with tongs. For a hidden tang knife, all that is needed is a gentle taper to the tang, in both width and thickness. The steps for the guard or spacer can be easily cut in with a file or grinder later.

The blade forging is now complete. But, there is yet another step. All of the heating, cooling and hammering have left the internal structure of the steel pretty messed up. To straighten things out, a step known as normalizing is required. To normalize the blade, heat it to 1550F and allow it to cool in air. This is usually done twice, just to make sure it was done correctly. This step can be completed

The blade bevel is forged using glancing blows near the edge of the anvil.

The point is forged at the far edge of the anvil. This allows the forging of a fine point without hitting the anvil with the hammer.

The bevel is continued back towards the tang. Forging the bevel will leave th edge a little wavy.

The taper is forged with the bar flat on the anvil face.

The edge and spine are smoothed and blended as the final bevel forging step.

After the bar is pointed and tapered, the bevel is forged, starting at the tip.

The blade is cut from the main bar by using the hardie.

The tang is forged as a simple taper. The steps and shoulders are easy to grind in later.

in a forge or kiln. The usual practice around here is to do it in the forge first, then when time is available later, do it again with the kiln.

The blade has now been forged and normalized. Since this Damascus is made from an oil hardening steel, it will still be too hard to file and drill. The blade must be annealed, or softened. This will also stet the internal structure up for proper hardening and tempering later. To anneal the O1/L6 Damascus, heat the blade in a kiln set to 1380F for one hour. The temperature is then ramped down to 950F over the next 12 hours, or a cooling rate of 35 degrees per hour. After the blade reaches 950F, the cooling rate is not important.

Author forges a blade on a 500lb anvil with a 2.2lb Peddinghaus hammer.

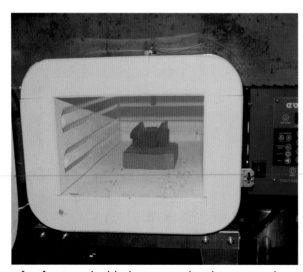

After forging, the blade is normalized in an Evenheat KF22.5 kiln. (Note: Forging temperature is not accurate in the photos.)

The finished blade forging, normalized, annealed, and ready for grinding.

The blade with most of the forge scale removed.

The blade after initial clean up with the 60 grit belt.

The blade after 60 grit grinding.

When flattening the ricasso and cleaning up the blade taper, be careful to keep your fingers away from the top wheel on the platen.

## Blade grinding

The first step in grinding the blade is to remove all the scale formed during forging. This is usually done with a 60 grit belt, on the two-inch rubber-faced wheel, at the bottom of the grinder platen. The plan is to just remove the bulk of the forge scale and some of the pits. The detail work is left for the flat surface of the platen.

After the blade is cleaned up, the ricasso area of the blade is flattened and trued. As the blade was forged slightly over-sized, now is the time to get the blade thickness down. Starting with a 60 grit belt, the ricasso area is ground down to about 0.005 inches oversize. Special attention is given to comparing the thickness at the top and bottom of the ricasso. Be sure the thickness is within 0.002 inches. It will make fitting the guard or spacer much easier later. During this step, the taper in the blade's thickness is defined as well.

Making the Using Knife

The spine is smoothed on the 60 grit belt

The edge is smoothed on the 60 grit belt. Remove about 0.010 inches of material to allow for decarburization during forging.

The blade bevel is ground, freehand, with the cutting edge up.

Very little shaping is done with the 220 grit Klingspor belt. The primary purpose is to remove 60 grit scratches.

On the belt sander, you can't see what you are grinding while the blade is on the belt. Progress is checked often.

The blade at a 220 grit finish.

The roughing of the Tang is done with a 60 grit belt running at high speed.

The ricasso thickness is checked often to be sure the top and bottom stay the same measurement.

Two hardened bars of steel are clamped to the blade. This simple tool makes cutting square shoulders an easy task.

Grinding the bevel is next. The blade is held edge up on the grinder platen. Since the blade was forged with a taper in the thickness of the spine, the stock removal practice of scribing a center line down the edge would be quite difficult. Things are just kept centered by eye. Care is taken to be sure the edge is centered and the right and left sides of the blade are mirror images of each other. Once again, with the 60 grit belt, everything is left slightly oversize.

If the blade were to be heat treated in a forge or regular kiln, the heat treating would usually be done at a 60 grit finish. This would leave some extra steel to allow for additional grinding. This grinding would be required to remove scale and decarburization formed during heat treating. Since this blade is to be heat treated using a salt bath, there won't be any scale or decarburization. The blade can be at 240, or even 400 grit for heat treating in a salt bath.

The next step is to go over everything again with 220 grit. This cleans up the 60 grit scratches and finalizes the dimensions.

After the blade grinding, the tang is profiled and tapered. Using the platen and a 60 grit belt,

The blade is ready for heat treating. It has a 220 grit finish.

The blades, with wire handles, austenize in the 1500 degree salts for 10 minutes.

this is quick work. Lay out the shoulders for the guard/spacer. Grind nearly up to the line. The tang should be tapered so that the line for the spacer is the thickest part of the entire blade. This makes fitting the spacer much easier.

A filing jig is used to finish the shoulders of the blade for the spacer. Two hardened bars of steel, with guide pins, are clamped to the blade. A file is used to remove the excess metal. It is a good idea to be sure the junction where the tang joins the blade is slightly radiused. This will minimize the possibility of stress cracking where the blade and tang meet.

If the blade is large or required a lot of grinding, there will be internal stresses built up from all the grinding, filing and drilling. To stress-relieve the blade, heat it to 1250F for one hour and allow it to air cool. For a small or simple blade, this step may be skipped. If a lot of heat was generated while grinding, it needs to be done.

## Heat treatment

Heat treating is where the "soul" of the knife is born. The ultimate strength, ability to be sharpened, and edge holding ability are largely determined at this point. Since this step is so critical, it is important to use the very best equipment available. The blade will be heated in molten salt bath and then quenched and tempered in a second salt bath. This is not to say that good results can't be obtained by

After 10 minutes in the 1500 degree salt, the blade is removed and quickly quenched.

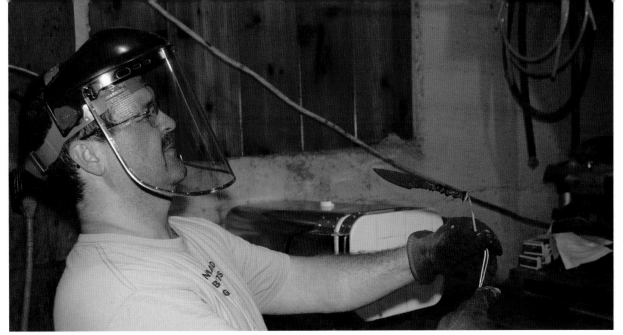

After removal from the 430 degree salt, the blade is checked for straightness. At 430 degrees, the blade hasn't hardened yet, and may be straightened if necessary.

The blades are returned to the low temperature salt for tempering, three times.

using a torch, forge or kiln and a bucket of oil. But, when the goal is to make the best knife possible, use the best equipment available.

With the proper equipment, heat treating is pretty straightforward. The high temperature salt, a sodium chloride solution, is heated to 1500F. After the salt is up to temperature, the blade is hung on a wire and immersed in the salts. After ten minutes the blade is pulled from the salts and quickly quenched in the low temperature salts. A rapid agitation is used during the quench to hasten the cooling of the blade.

The low temperature salt is for cooling, or quenching, the blade. It is a sodium nitrate/nitrite

With the blades in a small dewar, the liquid nitrogen is carefully added.

solution specifically designed for this application. The procedure used here is known as martempering. It is probably better called "marquenching" because the detail is in the quenching, or cooling, part of the process.

In martempering, after the blade is heated to 1500F, it is cooled quickly forcing it to harden.

The martempering procedure is to interrupt this cooling at 430F. This is because at 430F the blade hasn't hardened yet. It has only "promised" to harden due to the rapid rate of cooling to below 1000F. The blade actually hardens as it cools from 430F to room temperature.

Interrupting the quench at 430F does some wonderful things. As the blade soaks at 430F, the temperature equalizes throughout the blade. The edge, back and tang are all the same temperature. Then, as the blade cools from 430F down to room temperature in air, it will do it slowly and evenly. This gives a hardened martensite structure with very low internal stress. The resulting blade will have 20 to 25% increased tensile and impact strength, as compared to one quenched in 150 degree F oil, with no loss in hardness. It is also possible to straighten a slightly warped blade as it is cooling to room temperature. The actual hardening is happening as the blade cools from 430F.

After the blade has cooled to room temperature, it is actually too hard and brittle to make a good knife. The blade must be slightly softened, or tempered. It is very convenient that there is a salt pot already running at 430F. It makes a wonderful tempering location. Allow the salt pot to cool to 385F, and drop the blade in on a wire. After one hour, the blade is removed and cooled in water.

The next step is somewhat controversial. After the first temper, an option is to freeze the blades in liquid nitrogen. While this step is not essential for simple steels, it does seem to help. The freezing of

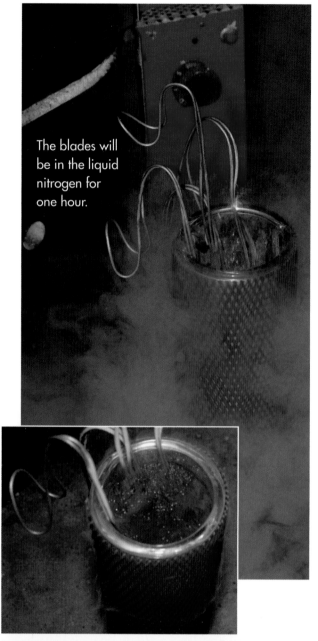

The blades will be in the liquid nitrogen for one hour.

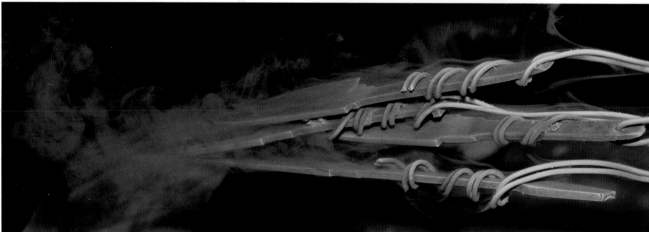

After the blades are removed from the liquid nitrogen, they are allowed to reach room temperature slowly.

The heat treated blade is tested for proper hardness. When the heat treat technique and material are known, tensile and impact strength values can be derived without destructive testing. The final hardness is 61 HRC.

simple tool steel blades doesn't seem to improve their edge holding ability. Yet, the frozen blades do tend to have an increased dimensional stability, and increased impact and tensile strength.

For the liquid nitrogen freeze, place the blade in a wide-mouth dewar, and pour the liquid nitrogen in slowly. There is a lot of boiling and fuming as the dewar and blade cools to -321F. Once the blade has cooled to the temperature of the nitrogen,

the boiling stops. The blade is kept in the liquid for one hour. It is then removed from the liquid nitrogen and allowed to slowly warm back to room temperature.

After the liquid nitrogen step, the blade is tempered two more times, one hour each, in the 385F salt pot. The blade is now ready for final grinding and polishing. The hardness is 61HRC.

The entire process looks like this:

1 Heat blade to 1500F in molten salts – hold 10 minutes.

2 Quench blade in 430F salts with a rapid agitation – hold one minute at 430F.

3 Air cool to room temperature.

4 Temper in molten salts – 385F, one hour, then cool to room temperature.

5 Freeze in liquid Nitrogen – one hour, slowly warm to room temperature.

6 Temper in molten salts – 385F, one hour, then cool to room temperature.

7 Temper in molten salts – 385F, one hour, then cool to room temperature.

## Final grinding

After heat treating, the blade is ready for final grinding and sanding. Since the blade was at a 220 grit finish during heat treating, we can start right

The edge is blended in to the main bevel by using the slack belt above the platen. An x weight belt makes this easier.

After using the belt sander to 400 grit, the blade is hand sanded with 600 grit open coat sand paper. A steel bar is used for a sanding block. This is usually done wet, using water as a lubricant.

The blade has been hand sanded to 600 grit by hand and is ready for Etching in the Ferric Chloride solution.

off with 400 grit. If there is very minor shaping to do, 220 grit is a better place to start.

Starting with the ricasso, now is the time to make sure the area where the blade meets the handle is perfect. Be sure the ricasso/tang junction measures the same in thickness, top and bottom. The discoloration from heat treating makes it easy to see when all the 220 grit scratches are gone. Continue with the clean up of the blade bevels and spine.

Before the final hand sanding of the blade, blend in the start of the cutting, or honing, bevel. A completely finished flat ground blade is actually only flat to within 1/16 inch or so of the cutting edge. The blade begins a gentle radius to the edge at this point. Since the edge was ground to a 0.010-inch thickness at the edge, there is not much blending to do.

For blending the edge, use the slack belt part of the belt sander. Running slowly, with a worn out 400 grit belt, a very gentle rocking motion will blend things in nicely. Be careful not to lift the blade spine very far off of the belt. It is easy to get too obtuse of an angle.

After the 400 grit work, a little hand-sanding is in order. Using 600 grit silicon carbide sand paper and a sanding block, sand out the 400 grit scratches. Finish with the 600 grit scratches running the length of the blade.

# Etching and polishing

To bring out the Damascus patterning in the blade, it must be etched. For the O1/L6 Damascus in this blade, ferric chloride is the simplest and best way to go. The ferric chloride seems to work best when diluted 50% with distilled water.

Be sure the blade is clean of all oil and fingerprints. Then:

1 Coat any areas you do not want to etch with fingernail polish.

2 Hang the blade vertically in the ferric chloride solution (usually blade tip down).

3 Leave the blade in the solution for two minutes. Slightly longer times are required if the ferric chloride solution is old or cold.

4 Remove the blade from the solution.

**5** Rinse the blade with hot water.

**6** Dry the blade with a paper towel.

**7** Lightly hand sand the blade with 1500 - 2000 grit sandpaper.

**8** Repeat steps 2-7 until desired depth and contrast are achieved.

**9** Optional – After the last etch, do not dry or sand the blade. Instead, place the blade directly in boiling water for 10 minutes. This seems to make the black more permanent.

**10** Remove any fingernail polish with acetone.

**11** Lightly sand the blade with worn-out 2000 grit sandpaper.

**12** Polish the blade using a soft cotton cloth and Simichrome polish. Or, buff the blade very gently with a very fine polishing compound.

**13** Coat the blade with a good, non-evaporating gun oil or hard wax such as Ballistol Wax.

At this point the blade is finished, except for final sharpening and polishing. Spacer and handle fitting is next. Before fitting the spacer, tape the blade with masking tape to avoid cutting yourself and to keep from scratching the blade.

The blade turns very dark in the Ferric Chloride. Gentle hand sanding will reveal the Damascus pattern.

Left: Between etches, and after the final etch, the blade is gently sanded with 2000 grit sand paper.

The blade is finished and ready for fitting the handle

# Spacer fitting

In keeping with the made-in-Michigan theme of this knife, the spacer is to be made from a piece of natural float Copper from the Keewenaw Peninsula. The copper has been forged flat and ground square on the front, back and two sides.

Cutting the slot for the tang can be done in a number of ways. The easiest is to use a milling machine. It is possible to fit a spacer or guard just as closely by hand, using files. The milling machine just makes the task easier and faster.

After the copper material is prepared, a center line is scribed, as well as the top and bottom limits of the tang. This gives a visual reference to help keep things in line. The copper is then put in the milling machine vise and checked to confirm it is flat and square in the vice.

Float Copper is "gummy" to machine, even after work hardening by cold forging. Because of this, it is a good idea to get most of the material out of the way using a drill bit, then use a milling cutter for the detail work. The slot on this knife should have a final width of 0.106 inches. A 3/32-inch milling cutter will be used for the final clean-up cuts. The material removal pre-drilling will be done with a 3/32-inch drill bit as well. That gives a line of holes that are 0.012 inch undersized, compared to the width of the tang.

When drilling the holes on the milling machine, start the holes with either a spotting drill or a combined drill/countersink. That will keep all the holes in a nice straight line. If the holes are started with a drill bit, they will tend to wander off center a

The holes are drilled to remove the bulk of the material.

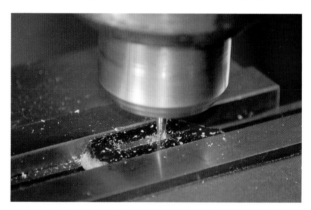

A 3/32 carbide milling cutter is used to open the slot to final dimensions.

The "Squashed Pipe Tool" is used to gently tap the spacer in to place. Tap the end of the pipe with a hammer. Don't use the pipe itself as a hammer.

After fitting with the Squashed Pipe Tool, the ricasso shoulders are scribed. The excess material is removed with a small hand engraving tool.

The front face of the finished spacer. The ricasso shoulder insets are clearly seen.

Below: A number 2 combined drill and countersink is used to start the holes, and keep them in a straight line.

A center line and top and bottom tang limits are marked on the front of the spacer. Dykem blue is used to make things easier to see.

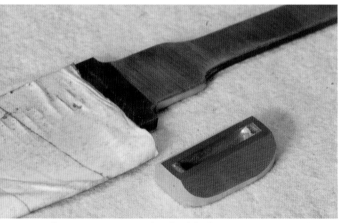

The spacer is 99% finished before handle assembly.

little. There is only 0.006 inch on either side of the line of holes to clean up. If the drill wanders at all, it will be impossible to make a nice looking slot. Start the holes with a #2 drill/countersink. Drill a pilot hole with a #44 (0.086-inch) drill bit. Drill the final hole with a 3/32-inch bit.

After the holes are drilled, the milling cutter is used to clean things up. The slot is opened to 0.105 inch by shifting the cutter 0.0055 inch each side of center. The idea is to have the milled slot 0.001 inch narrower than the tang. The final fit is achieved by gently driving the spacer on with a home-made squashed pipe tool.

It is difficult to have the top and bottom blade shoulders fit perfectly against the spacer material. The best solution for this was demonstrated by Brian Lyttle several years ago. After the spacer is tapped in place, carefully scribe the front face of the spacer around the top and bottom of the ricasso. Remove the spacer from the blade. Using a small engraving tool, remove about 0.003 of the front face of the spacer, being careful to stay well inside the lines. After the material is removed, put the spacer back on the blade and give it a good

The profile of the tank is traced on to the maple block. A centerline and top and bottom limits are drawn on the end.

smack using the squashed pipe tool. This will very slightly inset the blade shoulders in to the front of the spacer material. Carefully clean up the deformed material on the front of the spacer with some 400 grit sand paper on a flat surface.

The spacer is then ground and profiled to its nearly finished shape. This will keep the amount of grinding, and resultant heat, to a minimum during the final shaping of the handle. The front face of the spacer is completely finished at this time.

## Fitting the handle

There are several ways to fit a hidden tang handle. For this knife, the hole for the tang will be hollowed out of a solid block of maple. Doing this without splitting the handle in two halves, as with a mortised hidden tang, will eliminates having a large glue seam all the way around the finished handle.

Start by squaring up the handle material. Everything is easier to lay out and work on if the handle block is square and flat. Use a small machinists square to check that the end for the blade is square with the sides. With a sharp pencil, draw the profile of the tang on the side of the handle material. On the end mark a center line and the top and bottom limits of the tang.

Choose a drill bit that is slightly larger than the thickness of the tang. About 0.050 inch oversize is about right.

The handle block is aligned so the drill bit is parallel to the top of the tang.

Using a drill press to drill the handle block helps to keep everything straight. With the handle block in the drill press vice, angle the block so the drill bit runs parallel to the top of the tang. Set the depth stop or mark the drill bit so the hole isn't drilled too deeply. Carefully drill the hole. Move the drill bit in small steps, pulling the bit out to clear the wood chips. After drilling the hole that runs parallel to the top of the tang, tip the block in the vice and drill a hole that runs parallel to the bottom of the tang.

The next step is to remove the wood between the top and bottom holes. Split the angular difference between the top and bottom holes, and drill out any remaining wood. Holding the wood in the vice, it is pretty easy to move the block back and forth and clean out the excess material.

Make a trial fit to be sure the tang goes into the handle completely. If it doesn't, a little more drilling is in order. The drill bit can be gently used as a pseudo-router to help clean out the hole. Be careful to keep the hole for the tang as small as possible. Most knife makers have horror stories of cutting into the hole for the tang while finishing a handle.

Be sure to check the junction between the back of the spacer and front of the handle. Any gaps will become unsightly glue lines after the handle is glued and finished. Slide the blade, spacer and handle together. Hold everything together with a little hand pressure. Check for gaps with a bright light.

Once the tang has been fit in the block, profile the handle with a band saw and/or belt sander. Still having the profile of the tang drawn on the handle block will help avoid cutting in to the hole drilled for the tang.

With the blade spacer and handle block together, draw a line around the perimeter of the spacer. This gives a guide for roughing out the sides of the handle. Many simple knives have flat handles. Consider giving the handle a little flare, taper, or swell in the center. It looks better and is usually more comfortable in the hand.

## Gluing the handle

The choice of which glue to use is largely personal preference. Most of the available glues and epoxies will work just fine. Since a vent hole wasn't drilled while making the hole for the tang, it is a good idea to choose a glue that is quite runny or has a low viscosity at room temperature.

Some epoxies have the tendency to swell after curing; mostly, these are the five-minute varieties. Brownell's Acraglas avoids the swelling problem. It was designed to use in the fitting of gun stocks. It is also very runny and has a long set-up time. Unless you are in a hurry, Acraglas is a good choice.

Grind a few small notches in the edges of the tang. This gives the glue something to set in to, keeping the tapered tang from coming out of the handle.

To get things ready for final assembly, clean all the surfaces to be glued with your favorite

Everything is de-greased with acetone and ready for assembly. A black spacer has been added to keep the copper spacer from turning the maple handle green.

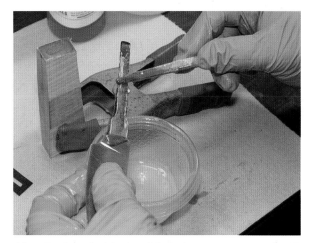

After the handle block is filled, the tang is coated with Acraglas.

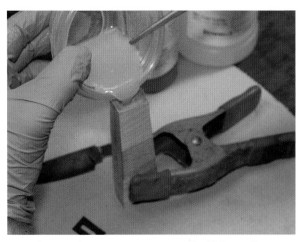

Mixed Arcaglas is very runny. Air bubbles will rise to the top.

The gluing is complete. The excess glue is wiped off with paper towels dampened with acetone.

cleaner/de-greaser. Acetone works well for this. Be sure to wear gloves and work with adequate ventilation

Gluing everything together is pretty simple with this hidden tang construction. Mix up enough glue to completely fill the hole in the handle. This will give enough excess to assure everything is well coated. With Acraglas, the ratio is one part hardener to four parts resin.

After the glue is mixed, fill the hole in the handle with the glue. Allow it to stand for a little bit to be sure all the air bubbles have risen to the top. Assemble the spacer on the blade. Coat the tang and back of the spacer with the glue. After everything is filled and coated, push the entire assembly together. Wipe off the excess glue and stand the knife with the blade vertical. Gravity will keep things together if the parts were fit with care.

An interesting thing happens at this point. Capillary action will draw the glue up between the spacer and the blade. This effectively seals the joint between the blade, spacer and tang. If there are large gaps from sloppy fitting, it is a good idea to coat the slot in the spacer and tang with glue before assembly.

As the glue comes up between the blade and spacer, it should be kept wiped off. As the glue starts to set up and get "stringy," the capillary action will stop. At this point, use a paper towel dampened with acetone to do the final cleaning.

## Handle finishing

Now that the knife is assembled, all that is left is the final shaping and blending of the handle and spacer.

Starting with a 60 grit belt, finalize the shape of the handle and blend it to the spacer. There shouldn't be much material to remove. Most of that was done earlier, before gluing. After the 60 grit belt, continue to 220 and 400 grits. As with grinding the blade, very little material should be removed with these finer grits. Their primary purpose is to remove the scratches from the previous grit. The slack belt portion of the sander is used often to keep everything smooth and blended.

Final sanding is done by hand. Using 400 grit sandpaper, the entire handle is sanded and smoothed. A shoe-shine action is often used to remove facets and keep them from forming. The final sanding is done with the grain and 600 grit paper.

Several different wood finishes are available for the knife maker. As usual, each has advantages and disadvantages. For ease of use, and maintenance, oil finishes are popular. Birchwood Casey Tru-Oil Gun Stock Finish does a good job with dry woods such as maple and walnut. Home made combinations of lemon oil and beeswax are great for everything, but especially for oily and tropical woods.

After the handle finish has been applied and is dry, the final "sheen" is given to the handle. There are those who prefer a glossy handle. Buffed

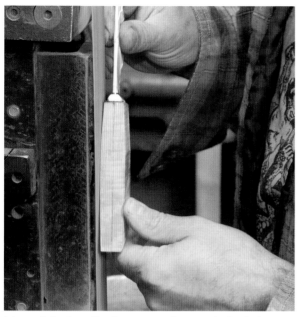

Most of the handle shaping is done with the belt sander. A center line has been drawn on the handle to help keep things centered.

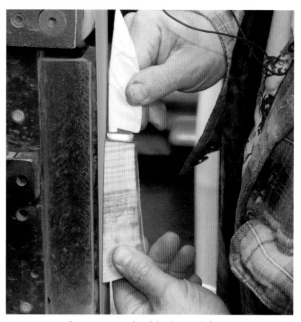

Tape is used to protect the blade and fingers during most of the handle work.

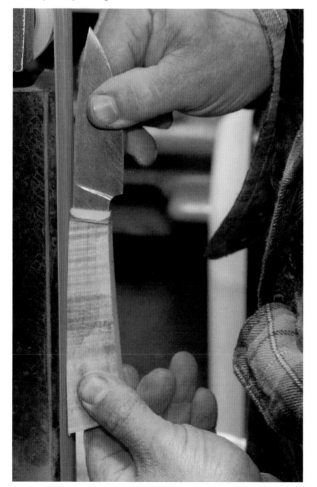

Sometimes the tape gets in th eway and must be removed for a short time.

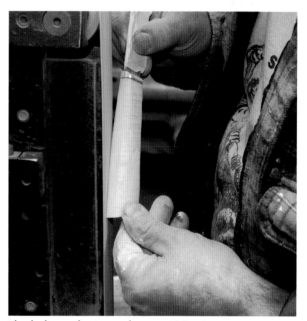

The belt sander is used up to 400 grit.

handles are often seen on knives that have CA, or super glue, type finishes. The glossy handles are fine, but tend to be slippery. Many of the "tactical" knives use a bead blasted finish. That is good too, but the bead blaster would really chew up this maple handle. A good compromise is to rub everything down with 0000 steel wool. Simply finish with the direction of the grain to avoid a scratchy looking finish.

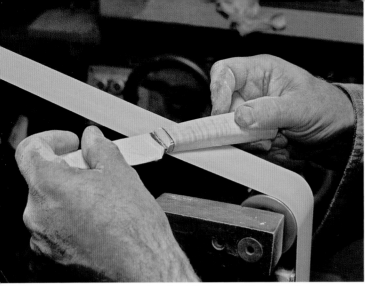

Working on the slack belt simplifies blending the different angles. A J weight, flexible belt is great on compound curves.

Working close to the wheel, the belt is effectively tighter. This makes is easier to keep straight lines straight.

# Sharpening

The blade had most of the edge bevel formed and blended before etching. There is only the final touch-up to do on the edge. Actually, this is usually done after making the sheath. There is less chance of cutting yourself or damaging the edge if you save the final sharpening for last.

Before etching, the edge was blended on the 400 grit slack belt and then further refined by hand sanding. The etching process continued the refinement of the edge by a combination of the action of the ferric chloride and the hand sanding with 2000 grit sand paper. The edge at this point was actually quite sharp, with a fairly aggressive tooth, due to the topography of the Damascus patterning. Many knife makers will deliver the knife with this etched edge. It is not a bad thing, but the edge can be even sharper with a little work on the stones.

How is the final edge angle determined? There are a lot of gizmos to help with this. These guides will clamp to the back of the blade, with or without running a bar through a guide system. For the most part they work fine, saving a lot of hassle in learning skills that will serve for a lifetime. It is not difficult at all to learn to see the different sharpening angles. Once you have established a baseline technique, you can decrease the angle a little for delicate knives, and increase the angle for the rough use knives.

Using an X weight, or stiff belt, helps to avoid undercutting the transitions between wood and metal.

A "shoe shine" motion is used to smooth and blend the handle. Used 2x72 belts are great for this. Changing the tension on the sandpaper helps to get various shapes and curves.

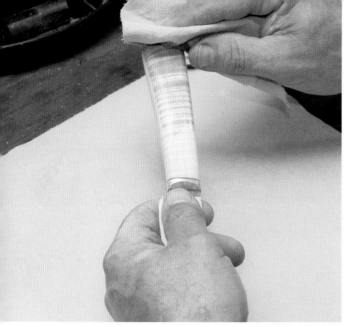

The Birchwood Casey Tru-Oil is applied with a paper towel.

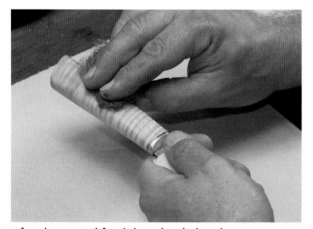

After the Tru-Oil finish has dried, the gloss is removed with 0000 steel wool.

The angle of the cutting edge is described as the "included angle." The measurement is from one side of the blade to the other. Some of the gizmos measure from the centerline of the blade to one side. So, the included angle is two times the angle from the centerline of the blade to one side. Just be certain of the reference point used when you are talking about edge angles.

Here is an easy way to get the honing angle in the ballpark without jigs or gizmos. Measure the width of the blade from the spine to edge. In the case of this knife the width is 1.12 inches. Divide this number by four. For this knife the blade width divided by four is 0.28 inch. This number (0.28 inch) is the height the center of the spine should be held off of the stone to get an included angle

of 29 degrees at the edge. This is a good angle for "slicers" and delicate use knives. Dividing the width of the blade by three, instead of four, kicks the angle up to 39 degrees, a good angle for rough stuff knives. In the case of this knife, holding the center of the spine off the stone 0.373 inches will result in a 39 degree final angle on the edge.

For perspective, most straight razors are honed in the 16 to 18 degree range. Commercial razor blades are often honed with up to a 25 degree angle. Fine chef's knives are in the 25 to 30 degree range. Heavy duty knives may have edge angles of up to 60 degrees.

If the Damascus etching is deep, a fair amount of metal must be removed to get down to the bottom of the etching. A Spyderco medium grit ceramic stone works well for this. Simply set the angle you want and slide the blade across the stone. The motion used is similar to what would be done if you were trying to cut a slice off the top of the stone. Use the same number of passes on both sides of the blade. Begin the metal removal with with gentle down pressure on the blade. As the bevel nears completion, only the weight of the blade is used on the stone. This step is finished when all the dark layers of the Damascus are completely gone from the edge of the blade.

Switching to the Spyderco fine grit ceramic stone completes the honing. Just as with the grinding and sanding above, the purpose of the fine grit stone is only to remove the scratches left by the medium grit stone above.

The edge is finished by gently stropping the edge on clean denim. The motion is the same as on the stones, only the blade is pulled away from the edge, or backwards. This removes any remaining burs and cleans the micro-teeth on the cutting edge.

As with most skills, sharpening may seem difficult at first. Practice and patience will lead to learning a skill few possess. Walk around a major knife show sometime. Ask to pick up the knives. Check the edges. Very few knives will be truly sharp, even on the tables of well known makers. That's sad.

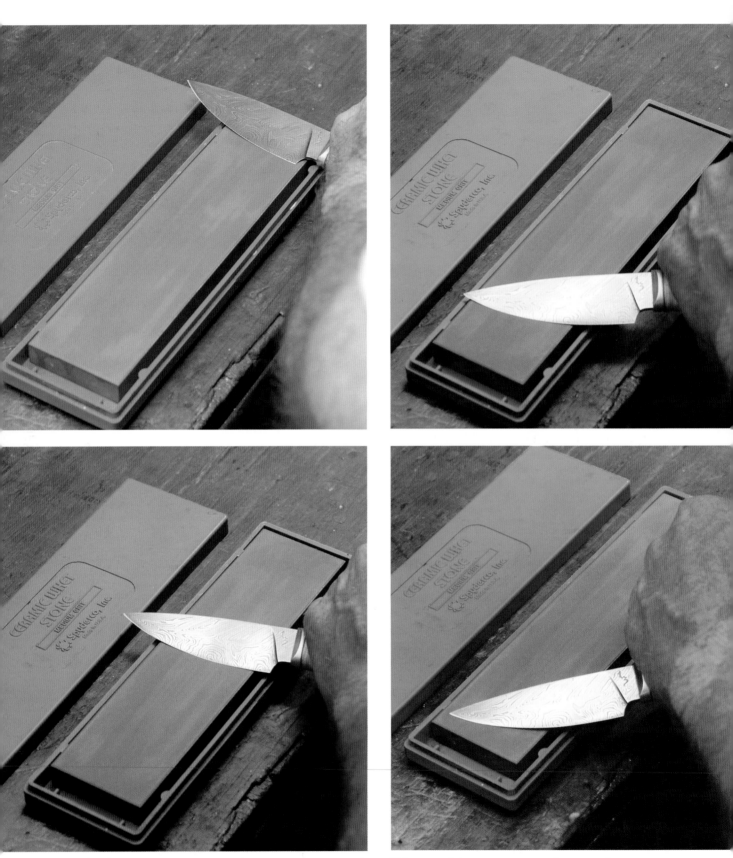

The sharpening motion is similar to "trying to cut a slice off the top of the stone." A Spyderco medium grit stone is used for the initial work. The fine and ultra-fine grits provide the finishing touches.

# The sheath

The sheath for a using knife can take many forms. As with the knife, it may be simple or elaborate as long as it does the job well. The choices of type and carrying position are many.

Since this knife is to be an every day tool, it should be quick and easy to get at. For a right handed person, that usually means carried on the right side, or hip. The blade may be straight up and down, angled forward or angled back. Cross draw positions also work well. With cross draw sheaths, the blade is usually angled down and back, or sometimes parallel with the belt. The decision is a very individual one. Many will end up with more than one sheath. The events of the day, and wardrobe, influence which sheath is chosen for the day.

Pouch sheaths are common with small using knives. They are less bulky than other sheath styles and still give the blade and handle excellent protection. A pouch sheath is simply a piece of leather that has been wrapped around the back and spine of the knife. The edges of the sheath come together along the edge of the knife and are stitched together. A welt is usually inserted along the sown edge to protect the stitching from the sharp edge of the blade.

A pouch sheath for a small using knife usually does not have a strap or snap to keep the knife securely in the sheath. Careful fitting and wet forming of the leather provides enough pressure and friction on the handle to keep the knife securely in the sheath. There are, however, many creative leather workers who have come up with ingenious ways of securing small guard-less knives in their sheaths. A quick search on the internet will yield many ideas.

# Final details

The knife is now finished. All that is left is to enjoy carrying and using it every day. With most things of value, there is a level of maintenance required. As the blade is a laminate of carbon steel, it will tarnish with use. If the blade is wiped off after use and oiled, it will not rust or pit.

Keep the blade oiled with a good non-evaporating oil. If the knife is to be used on food, the oil should be something you wouldn't mind eating. Mineral, olive, canola and other similar oils work well. Ballistol is also very good and lasts a long time.

Tarnish and discoloration are a given with carbon steel blades. Many actually prefer the tarnished look, and prefer to allow the knife to "age gracefully." Others like to keep the knife looking brand new. To keep the knife looking new, simply polish the blade with Simichrome when tarnish appears. If the blade has been allowed to go beyond the lightly tarnished stage, a little more work will usually clean things up quite well. Gentle hand sanding with 2000 grit sandpaper will hit the high spots in the etched surface of the Damascus steel. Following that up with the Simichrome polish will usually have the blade looking near new. Don't forget to put on a protective coat of oil as the last step.

The leather sheath requires maintenance as well. As with fine shoes or boots, the leather should be kept as dry an clean as possible. Occasional cleaning, followed up with an application of a quality leather preservative, such as Obenauf's, will keep the sheath looking like new for years.

The "secret" to having a sharp knife with you all the time is to simply keep it sharp. Don't allow the blade to actually become dull before touching up the edge. A knife is far easier to keep sharp than it is to re-sharpen. Usually, a few passes on the Spyderco fine grit stone work very well for regular maintenance. If the knife has become too dull for the fine grit stone to be effective, drop back to the medium grit ceramic stone, reestablish the honing bevel, finish with the fine grit stone and denim strop.

Making a using knife can be quite a process. The materials, tools and techniques can be very simple and inexpensive, or complex and expensive. The most important thing is to do the very best you can, using the best materials and methods you have available. The result will be a knife that beckons to be put on every day, taken out and used.

# Making Patterns and Using a Pantograph

## by Allen Elishewitz

Fifty years ago, the pantograph was one of the most important machines in a mold shop. At the time, very few manufacturers could afford CNC machining centers, so they hired skilled machinists capable of using pantographs.

A pantograph is a manually-operated duplicating machine. Typically a pantograph has two sides, one for holding the pattern and one for cutting the parts. The pattern side usually uses a stylus to trace the template; the cutting side utilizes a collet or some sort of cutter fastener. Different manufacturers arranged the machines differently. Sometimes the tables are side by side, on other machines they are front and back, and I have even seen some that are top and bottom. These machines work by manipulating arms to duplicate, reduce or enlarge a pattern.

In the 1960s, these machines could easily cost upward of $60,000. Today, they are obsolete in modern mold shops, bringing the price as low as $500 to $2000.

Does this mean that the pantograph cannot produce quality work? No, we live in a different time with the efficiency of CNC machines that also require less manual labor and keep the cost down. For artisans that want to preserve the skills of handcraft, the pantograph is a wonderful tool to have. The art of hand made is all about the human factor; the fact that someone has to manually control and manipulate a machine to produce a result. Since everything has gone to computer controlled, integrated software and high tech equipment, a lot of knowledge on the use of a pantograph has been lost. I would like to share with you my approach and techniques in utilizing a pantograph for handmade knives.

## The Deckel GK-21

The machine demonstrated in this article is a Deckel GK-21. This pantograph is a little bit larger than the GK-12, which is really an engraving machine. The GK-21 has heavier arms so it can be used to remove metal as well as engrave.

Deckel is a German company and one of the leaders in the field of machine tools. The older Deckels have a round base for each table and the

A number of styluses, collets and end mills can be used on the Deckel GK-21. Notice the number of styluses in this holder; they are only for two end mills, so don't think you can get away with just one or two styluses per end mill.

The pattern table on the right of the Deckel GK-21, and work table is on the left. The stylus holder is on the right side while the spindle is above the work table. Three adjustments on the arms change the ratios. You must change each one of them according to the ratio or else your pattern will be leaning to the left or right, up or down. On each arm, I have made brackets (stops) so I can immediately go to 5:1 or 2:1 and repeat the exact spot I was at each time. If you do not have stops and you adjust your ratios, you will never come back to the exact location you were previously at. A neat little feature I have added to this machine, which is very simple to do, is two bags of lead shot laying on one of the arms. Each bag weighs about five to seven pounds and dampens the vibrations dramatically.

Z axis is located underneath the tables. My Deckel is a 1980s version near the end of the pantograph production; you can tell by the square columns under the tables and the location of the Z axis on the side of the table, which is more convenient to use.

The basic design feature of the GK-21 machine is that it transfers all three-dimensional tracer pen motions to the cutting tool, in the same direction and at preset duplicating ratio. The pattern or master and the work piece are always clamped in conjugated positions at roughly the same level, right in front of the operator, for maximum convenience and ease of operation. The pantograph will give a mathematically true reproduction of the template or pattern contours if the diameter of the tracer pen and cutter are selected in accordance with the duplicating ratio and if the points of tracer pen and cutter are in alignment with the axis of the horizontal pivoting shaft. The GK-21 can reduce or enlarge a pattern from 1:1.5 to 1:10.

The cutter spindle can be conveniently removed from its bayonet-type holder for maintenance. It runs in an adjustable, anti-friction bearing, designed for long life and high running accuracy. The speed of the GK-21 ranges from 475 to 20,000 rpm. The spindle top is provided with a combined coarse and fine vertical feed attachment, which allows the user to engage and retract the cutter when needed. The cutter tools are held by exchangeable spring collets.

There are numerous attachments for the Deckel pantograph, and it's amazing to me that these guys thought to use them on this machine. For example, there is a forming attachment that is standard on all Deckel GK-21s. On top of the spindle there is a cap that can be removed; a needle plunger is located beneath this cap. By attaching a forming guide on a forming guide holder, this forces the cutter in an up-and-down motion, allowing the user to cut in a convex shape. Another accessory is an electro-marking unit, which is attached in the spindle and is powered by 220V AC. It can etch and darken hardened steel. A rolling engraving attachment is one of the rarest attachments for the Deckel; it allows you to engrave radius surfaces by rotating the part in an arc. This is just a sampling of the possibilities.

For this project, we'll make the parts for a new model knife. But before we begin making chips with the pantograph, we need to design our knife and make patterns. Make a copy for all the parts that need patterns: blade, liners, bolsters and handles.

Making Patterns and Using a Pantograph

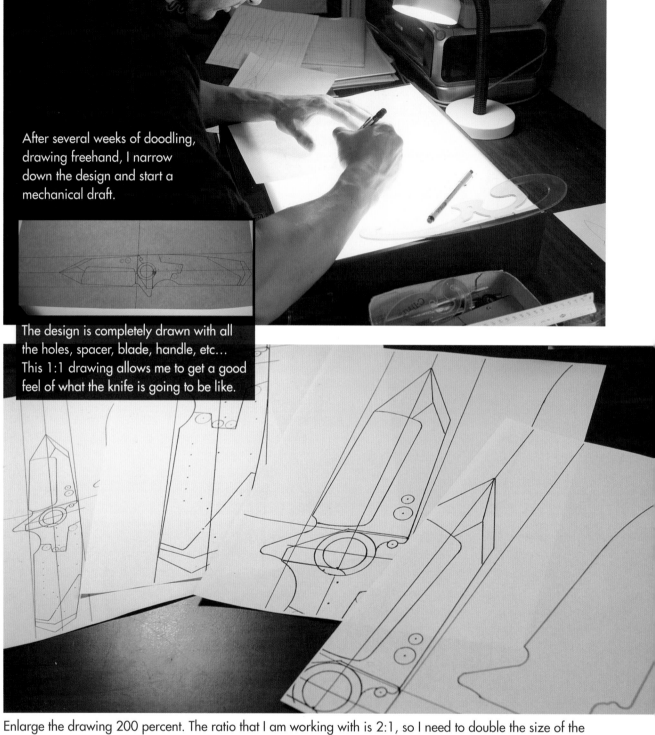

After several weeks of doodling, drawing freehand, I narrow down the design and start a mechanical draft.

The design is completely drawn with all the holes, spacer, blade, handle, etc... This 1:1 drawing allows me to get a good feel of what the knife is going to be like.

Enlarge the drawing 200 percent. The ratio that I am working with is 2:1, so I need to double the size of the original drawing. Some pantographs allow the user to duplicate 1:1, but the ideal setting would be 2:1 or 3:1. The advantage of a larger ratio than 1:1 is both mechanical and for precision. By changing the arms to a higher ratio, you gain a mechanical advantage over the cutter; the stylus/tracer pen will become much easier to move around the pattern, the accuracy or precision also improves due to the fact that you are reducing the error by the same ratio. For example, if you had a .050 hump that was a mistake, it will get reduced to .025 on a 2:1 ratio. I have used both 2:1 and 3:1 ratios for knifemaking, but I like the 3:1 better because of everything mentioned here. However I have abandoned this ratio and stuck with 2:1 because of the pattern size. If you have a 4-inch blade in a 2:1 ratio, that means your pattern is eight inches, a 3:1 ratio will bump your pattern to 12 inches. In some cases, I have had patterns so big they were almost hanging off the table!

Cut out the paper copies.

Put double-sided tape on 3/8-inch thick G-10.

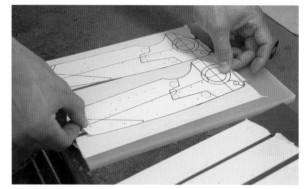

Lay the cutout enlargements on the tape.

Cut the G-10 on band saw.

On this pattern, drill 3/16-inch holes for every hole that would be drilled for a screw. I use this size because I have 3/16-inch locating pins that will be placed in these holes.

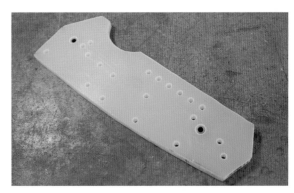

Press-fit drill bushings through the pivot pin and tooling holes. These holes get used the most during the knifemaking process, so by reinforcing them they will not get damaged from use.

Set up disk grinder at a 90 degrees angle and start grinding the G-10 to the lines of the patterns. Here, two patterns are stacked and held together by 3/16-inch pins in the various holes that were drilled.

Do the same thing to the blades. Machining serrations in various locations on the blade allows the option to serrate the blade if needed. The serrations are only machined a third of the way down; allowing the option to add or prevent serrations in a particular location.

Examine the blade pattern in the open and closed position.

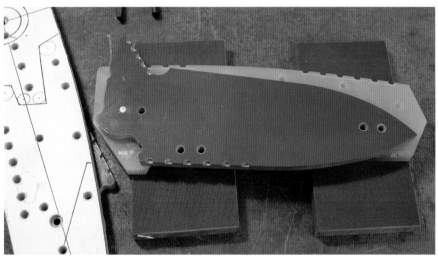

Begin to make fixtures to hold down the workpiece.

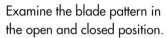

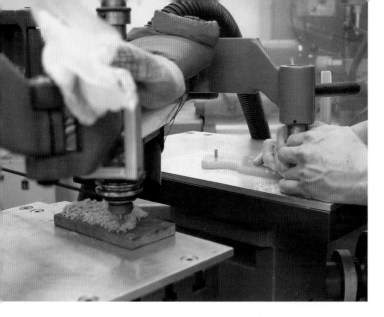

Blade's Guide to Making Knives

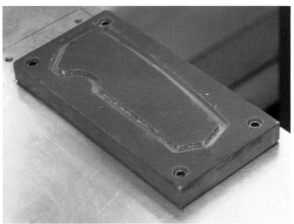

Trace the handle pattern and cut a profile on a G-10 block. This is where I will bolt down the liners to be machined. The channel is cut quite deep to allow the cutter more room to move while it is profiling the liners. It also gives a place for the chips to gather while the cutter is going around the workpiece.

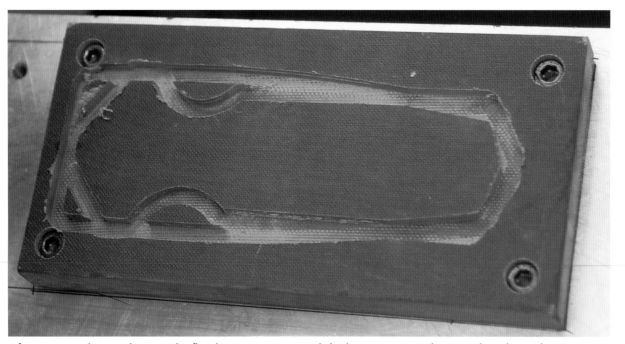

After you are done with one side, flip the pattern over and do the exact same thing on the other side. Now you have two mirror images on top of each other. This gives you the ability to flip the pattern from left to right which in turn gives you the option to make a right handed or left handed knife. Also, if some kind of special machining needs to be done on the left side, your fixture is already set up for this

Flatten the G-10 where it will come in contact with the liner. This produces a parallel and perpendicular surface to the table and the cutter.

Remove the pattern, and now it is time to bore out the tooling holes. One of them is the pivot pin, the other is some determined distance on the back end. The goal is to produce .250 holes in the G-10 fixture, using a .125 cutter. Remember that most end mills are not true to size; if you selected a .125 end mill, the actual cutting diameter could be .122. There is no way you can produce an end mill, sharpen it and maintain the same diameter. So by knowing this you must choose your stylus/tracer accordingly. Since I am using a .125 (but really .122), my final stylus is going to be .244. The first stylus that I use is .280 which is larger than my final stylus. This allows me to machine the material without overcutting the G-10. If you try to machine with the final stylus and you are removing a lot of material during each pass, you can overcut the material and the finish is not going to be the nicest you can get. Since I need to produce a .250 hole, I made a fixture out of steel that looks like a doughnut with a spud. The internal diameter of the doughnut is .50. The spud will fit in the hole for the pivot pin and the other tooling hole on the template; this allows you to place your liner on the G-10 fixture and mount it for your machining operation. Then I place the stylus in and trace the inside of the doughnut. This produced the round hole of the size I needed and I slowly inserted the cutter in the G-10 until it was all the way through.

The final result: a 1/4-inch pin slips snuggly in the holes.

Counter-bore the back side of the G-10 fixture to insert precision shoulder bolts and glue them in place. After the glue is hardened, place the fixture back on the pantograph and mount liners onto it.

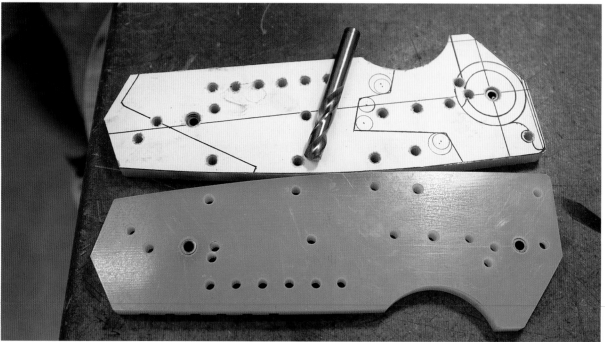

At this point, the two pairs of large G-10 liner patterns that are identical. On one of them I have removed the double-sided tape and paper pattern, the other pair is going to be made into bolsters and handle patterns. The pantograph cannot cut sharp corners; the corners can only be as sharp as the smallest endmill you can use. So what I do for corners is radius them. I usually use a 5/16-inch drill to create the radius. That will produce a .156 diameter during machining and I cannot use an endmill larger than this diameter; it would create gaps in my fit up. That is fine because I usually profile my patterns with a .125 endmill.

Drill the corners with a .3125 drill bit.

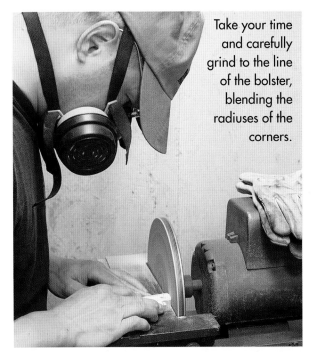

Take your time and carefully grind to the line of the bolster, blending the radiuses of the corners.

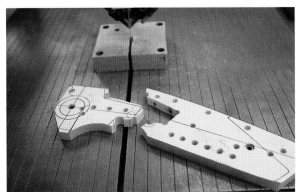

Start cutting the bolsters. I cut on the outside of the line. The advantage of using a .3125 drill bit is that my bandsaw blade is .250 wide; this allows me to cut and rotate when I am in the hole.

This is the part that is very similar to bedding the action of a rifle. You need to use Devcon Plastic Steel Liquid, a releasing agent and some tape.

Clean your parts thoroughly. Then apply the releasing agent on the G-10 pattern that you did not cut. Apply the releasing agent on the flat portion of the pattern which is directly under the bolster. Then apply the releasing agent on the inside edge of the bolster. You want to have the releasing agent on all surfaces that you do not want the resin to stick to. The releasing agent can be shoe polish or some kind of wax; I use Imperial Sizing Wax.

Making Patterns and Using a Pantograph

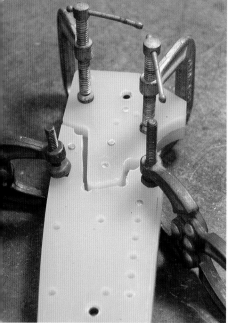

Put the handles together using 3/16-inch pins in the corresponding holes, the top and bottom handles should line up. Clamp them together; this will prevent the plastic steel from bleeding between the two G-10 layers.

Place tape on the edge of the pattern making a dam. I like to create a little pocket to cause the plastic steel to have an overflow. This will prevent the plastic steel from running out of the cavity and also making sure that you get the resin all the way to the edge without pockets or air bubbles.

Pour the Devcon into the channel, using a small stick push it down to insure there are no air pockets. Do not be stingy with it, allow it to have a slight overfill because it will settle and shrink down within 24 hours.

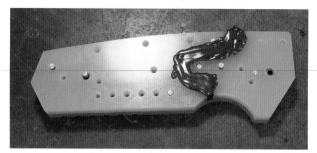

After 24 hours, the Devcon Liquid steel is hardened. Remove the clamps, tape and push out all the 3/16-inch pins. Then proceed to grind off the excess resin on the flats.

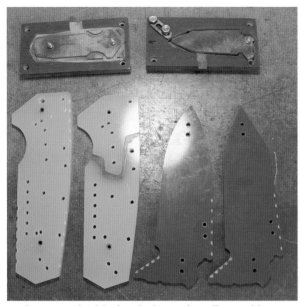

At this point the blades, bolsters, handles and liners patterns are complete, as well as the fixtures to hold the parts to be cut.

It is time to make the master patterns which will be used to scribe and drill on the various materials chosen to make the knife. I usually use .160 titanium to make these templates. In this photo I have done almost the exact same thing I did with the G-10 patterns, taping photocopies of the designs and cutting out the titanium.

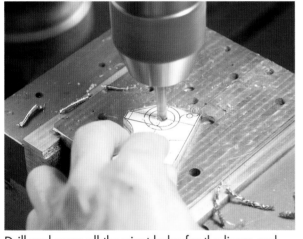

Drill and ream all the pivot holes for the liners and blade.

Machine the profile of the blade design with the corresponding blade pattern.

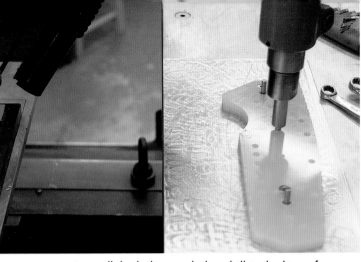
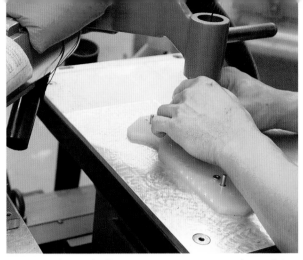

Spot all the holes needed to drill in the liners for screws, stop pins, detent ball, etc… It is an exact replica of the larger pattern made earlier. After spotting the liners, machine the profile the same as earlier with the blade.

Patterns used to create this particular model include fixtures to hold handles to be machined as well as liners and blades. The 2:1 G-10 patterns are used to machine the various components and the titanium liners are the exact size of the finished product. I have even gone as far as machining a pair of bolsters and handles out of G-10 so I can test the fit up of that particular pattern. This also allows me to have the exact shape of the bolsters and handles so I can orient them on various materials to achieve the best possible visual effect.

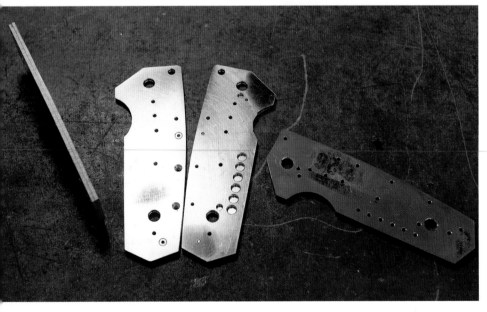

After making the patterns for this model, begin making the knife. For this project, I started with .070 titanium on which I scribed the liners and cut them on the band saw. After cutting, profile on the grinder as close to the line as possible but not going over. By doing this you remove a lot of material very fast, so you do not need to spend so much time on the pantograph. De-burr, straighten and lap the liners prior to drilling. Drill, ream and tap all the holes in the liners that are needed for the particular project.

After mating the left and right liners together, screw them together and make them one unit. Each numbered pair is then ready to be profiled on the pantograph. Buzz around the liners counter clockwise (conventional milling). After about two rotations, reverse direction and go clockwise (climb cutting, the cutter is "climbing up" the material). This particular technique produces a much nicer finish than conventional milling. You cannot start climb cutting without removing some material because the cutter would get jerked around and you could end up breaking your end mill. On a CNC mill this is not the case, but with the pantograph this is a concern.

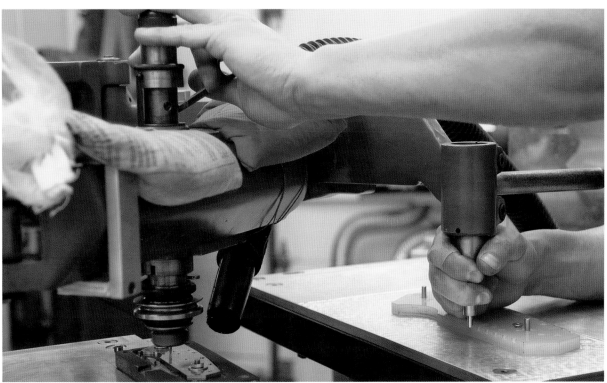

After profiling the liners, change the stylus and the end mill but leave the pattern and the part attached to the machine. Machine serrations in the liner using a .093 end mill with a .1875 stylus. The stylus drops into scallops machined during the pattern-building phase. The nice thing about this Deckel GK-21 is that the spindle can move up and down like a drill press. If you pull the lever on the top spindle you get a rapid descent of the cutter. If you rotate it clockwise you get a gradual descent of the cutter. This is a more controlled plunge than the rapid plunge. What I would do is insert the stylus into one of the scallops, hold it in place and drop the end mill until it cuts a crescent out of the liner; then pull back the cutter and go on to the next scallop. Repeat until all scallops are complete.

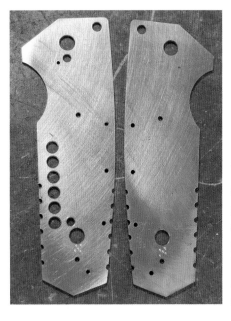

The liner is completely profiled with serrations machined. These liners are about 75% complete.

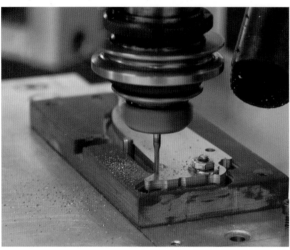

The same operation that was done on the liners can also be done on the blade. Remember you always want to start your profiling counterclockwise and clean it up clockwise. Just like the liner, you can add serrations to various locations on the blade. A knifemaker asked me once if it is faster to pantograph my parts than to just grind them to shape; the answer is no. Grinding your various components and ganging them up on the mill where you can machine 15-20+ liners at one time is always going to be faster than pantographing. What pantographing gives the user is consistency: Consistency of parts and of features. You are more consistent to machine serrations on a pantograph than on a mill. If you try to eyeball something on the mill, it will look like it was not calculated.

Blades and liners are not the only things you can use a pantograph for. The bolster is a part of the knife where the pantograph can really show its flexibility and advantages. I usually make a sacrificial liner that I can attach a bolster on while I am machining. Traditional bolsters are usually straight up and down; there are some "S"-shaped bolsters that you can do by hand, but it is tedious and time consuming. With the pantograph, the possible shapes for bolsters are endless. For me, this is where the true art of the pantograph comes into play. To make two different parts that can interlock without gaps is very difficult, there are many factors that can influence the final fit. Some materials can be overcut very easily, some materials have an elastic property and will not cut true, and some materials can wear down your cutter as you are machining, like carbon fiber which is very abrasive.

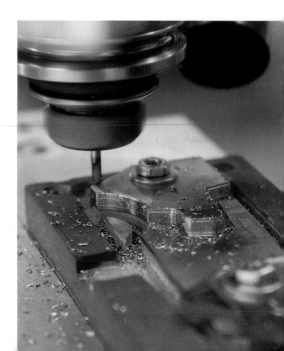

In order to have a very clean and precise part, I have found that using multiple styluses of descending sizes will produce the best results. On titanium or steel, I have noticed that a five-flutes end mill achieves a mill-like finish on what you are cutting, probably due to the extra flute or cutter that gives such a clean finish.

When preparing to machine a handle to fit up to the bolster, I machine an outline of the handle on the G-10 fixture. This gives me a reference to where I need to place the handle material. Most of the materials I deal with are flat on both sides; if you are working with stag, bone or ivory that has a curve on one side, you are going to have to flip your pattern to cut it on the left and right side since you cannot flip the material over.

For this knife I would like to have an ironwood handle placed behind the bolster. The slab of ironwood is oversized so I place it over my outline on the G-10 fixture. It's held in place with a C-clamp, and with a large stylus I slowly remove material. Decrease the diameter of the styluses to remove smaller amounts of the wood with each pass. Usually with handle materials, use a three- or four-flutes end mill. With a five-flutes end mill, the chips would end up clogging the narrow flutes.

After machining the handle material with the corresponding stylus, do not remove anything as it is time to check the fit of the bolster and handle. A lot of times it will be a tight fit. If you machine the bolster with a .125 end mill (really .122) and you finished it with a .244 stylus and do the exact same thing to the handle material, most of the time it will be a tight fit because some materials actually spring back. If it is a tight fit, use a smaller stylus so you can offset your cut to have a better fit. Remember that this is set up at 2:1! If you move the stylus two inches to the right, the cutter only moves one inch to the right. So if you reduce your stylus by .001 that means you are only undercutting .0005 and that doesn't make much of a difference. I have a series of stylus which I have made on my lathe in increments of .002 smaller than the cutters' sizes. This results in the best fit between the two parts.

Another technique of knifemaking that a pantograph can be utilized for is cutting chamfers around a frame and doing bolster-locks. Bolster-locks are very different from conventional bolstered knives. I developed this style in the mid 90s because in an attempt to achieve the classical look of a bolstered knife while maintaining the strength of a framelock. What I came up with is a thick titanium frame on which the handle has been machined away leaving a thin liner, with the front third of the liner remaining thick. This way a handle can be added to get the appearance of a knife with a bolster and handle material but on the back side, when you split your lock, part of the bolster is integrated with the liner in the lock area. To chamfer a piece of titanium that will be made into a bolster-lock, use a .3125 ball end mill offset so it produces a nice chamfer on the edge of the frame. There is no need to go around the entire handle, just the first third where the bolster will be located.

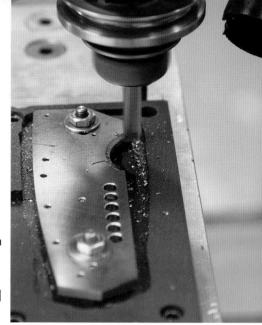

Notice the chamfer around the thick titanium frame and the cleanliness of the cut. This is achieved by doing two passes of climb cutting. Mark the frame with a sharpie for reference points to start and end cuts. You could do this by hand on a grinder, but it will never come out as clean and consistent as on the pantograph.

These operations are very similar to the earlier bolster process where I would trace the pattern and go down to a certain depth and decrease my stylus size to the desired size. The end result is an outline of the bolster leaving a webbing of titanium of about .070 thick.

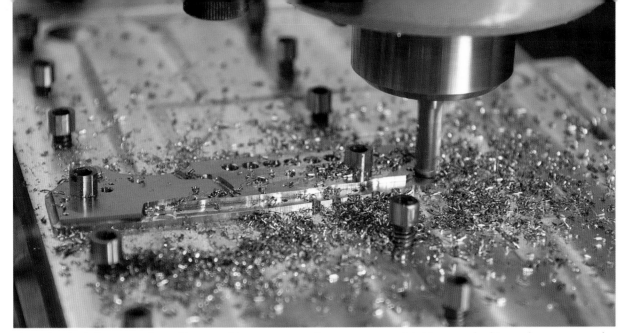

Place the thick frame on the milling machine to remove the excess material. You can do this on the pantograph, but it is much slower because you cannot remove as much material as with the mill. Mill down the frame to .070 to match the depth of the groove marking the edge of the bolster.

The final result is a liner with an integral bolster that has been chamfered all the way around. This work-in-progress shows the flexibility of the pantograph, its ability to work with a variety of materials and its use in creating various knife configurations. It is one of the more useful machine tools that a knifemaker can utilize and it is well worth spending the time to learn how to use it.

From this point on you would finish the knife like any other knife, contouring, polishing, grinding the blade, fitting up the lock and detailing everything. If you are careful enough in blending the handle material to the frame, you can actually swap handles between frames and everything will match up. That is a major advantage over profiling the parts by hand; the ability to interchange. I like it because it keeps my designs consistent. There are too many times I have seen the same models look completely different because the maker got carried away on the grinder or overcut thes material and had to compensate for the mistake. In concept, the fixtures, process and approach are very much like a CNC machine; the only difference is that a CNC machine's brain is a computer. The limitation of a pantograph is really the operator's imagination and ability. There are so many fixtures and tooling you can add to the Deckel to make it even more flexible in 2D and 3D. The only hurdle that you will encounter is the learning curve of how to set up the machine and how to fixture the parts (the most difficult problem that plagues all machinists); the rest is just coming up with ideas on how to achieve a particular technique. For me that is the fun part of using a pantograph!

The Tank has a tongue-and-groove style bolster and handle using two dissimilar materials: Mokuti from Chad Nichols and ironwood.

The Scout has a jigsaw puzzle handle construction with very difficult materials to work with. The super conductor is very gummy to machine, and the carbon fiber wears down the cutter.

The fancy Jekyll has a round tongue-and-groove Mokuti bolster and ivory handle. Notice how the pantograph has the ability to work with a variety of materials.

The Spatha is a classic, with titanium bolsters and wood handle in a jigsaw puzzle configuration.

For this knife, constructed with a bolster-lock, I chamfered the bolsters and machined the outline of the bolsters on the pantograph. This style of construction is completely different from a screwed-on bolster.

Notice the serrations on the bottom side of the liners.

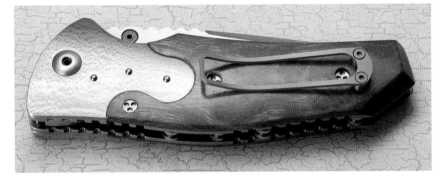

Serrations on the top of the liners and top of the blade give the knife more texture for better grip.

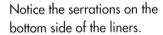

The pantograph created the flutes on this fancy folder. The groove in the blade was also done using the machine. The nice thing about making blood grooves or flutes on blades with the pantograph is that it can follow the contour of the blade. This gives a fancier, custom look to the knife, and it is also more difficult.

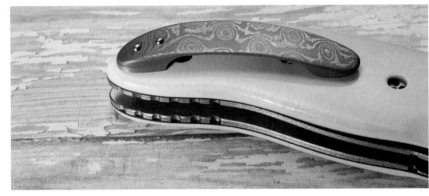

Making Patterns and Using a Pantograph

# Forging Steel from Raw Materials

## by Don Fogg

Wootz Bowie by Alfred Pendray

Bladesmithing is a fascinating craft. The process is primal and it seems to awaken a deep curiosity in those who work at it. With simple tools, bladesmiths can enter a whole new world, rich in history and full of mastery. We can appreciate the intuitive understanding of the ancient smiths when they discovered and worked iron into steel. Their secret processes, lost in time, have engaged smiths of every generation for thousands of years. It is a quest inspired by the beauty and power of the objects that remain, the priceless artifacts of mastery. For a growing number of smiths, the path leads them to the creation of steel from raw materials.

There are two basic ways for the bladesmith to make steel. The first is to carburize iron by smelting iron ore in a charcoal furnace, and the second is to melt iron or in a crucible charged with carbon and other ingredients. The result is two different products. From the furnace you get a bloom of iron with varying degrees of carbon content mixed. From the crucible, a bulat or cake of steel.

## The crucible method and wootz steel

In the crucible method, the iron is melted inside a crucible to produce a button or cake of steel that then must be forged into a bar. Depending on the chemistry of the cake, you can get a material with defined carbide structure historically referred to as wootz.

Wootz steel was first produced around 300 BC in India and traded across the ancient world. It had remarkable properties compared to steel made by other methods. The laminar carbide structure of the early blades produced a characteristic watered or crystalline pattern on the surface of the steel. Swords made of wootz steel were encountered by Western Europeans during the crusades around 1100 AD. They were called Damascus steel blades, referring either to the damascene effect of the watered steel or for the city of Damascus where they were produced. Wootz is often called the true Damascus, in contrast with mechanically welded pattern steel more commonly seen in Europe and the Far East.

Wootz was a metallurgical enigma to the West. Despite firsthand accounts of the production methods in India, attempts to reproduce it inevitably failed. It wasn't until the study of chemistry in the early 1800s that the composition of the original wootz steel was discovered to be an alloy of carbon and iron. Those early experiments with wootz lay the foundation for modern materials science and it remained a metallurgical mystery until the late 20th century when interest was revived by Dr. Cyril Stanley Smith in his book, *The Search for Structure.*

The mastery of wootz became a lifelong quest for Alfred Pendray, a bladesmith from Florida. Alfred introduced his work with crucible steel at a hammer-in hosted by Dr. Karl Van Arnum in Florida 1982. Al had made a cake of wootz steel and was attempting to cut it with a chop saw. You could see the blade on the chop saw wear away as it barely cut the cake. Comprised mostly of carbides, it was devilish material both to cut and to forge. Al persisted with his quest and after many years of experiments started to make modern wootz blades. He demonstrated cutting a silk scarf floating in the air at the Knifemakers Guild show in Kansas City, Missouri. His quest drew the attention of Dr. J. D. Verhoeven, metallurgist Iowa State University. Not satisfied with simply making steel, Al and Dr. Verhoeven began a long series of experiments to find what constituted the old wootz steels, and ultimately they were able to reproduce it. They have published several articles covering their research and hold a patent on the process they discovered.

What distinguishes wootz from other crucible steels is that it is ultra-high carbon, between one and two percent, and that it forms a laminar of iron and carbide. It is this laminated structure that shows as a pattern when the steel is etched and polished.

The pattern resembles pattern-welded steels, but on close examination it can be seen to be intra-crystalline segregation. It is the composition of superfine spheroidised carbides aligned in layers with the iron that make this steel so remarkable. Verhoeven and Pendray discovered that it is the micro-alloying elements, chrome, titanium and primarily vanadium, that create these unique properties. Equally important was the under-

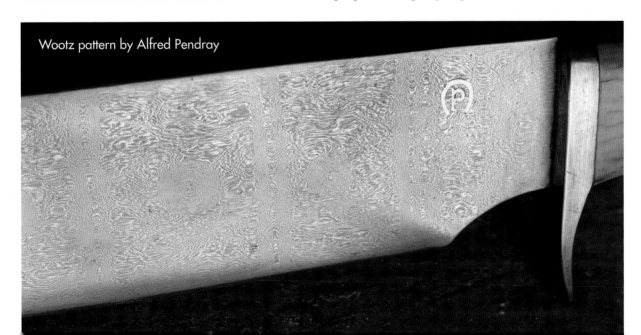

Wootz pattern by Alfred Pendray

standing of the detailed thermal cycle and cooling curves required to produce the carbide banding.

Their work together is quite remarkable. A country bladesmith from Florida working with a metallurgist from Iowa had solved a mystery that had eluded science for centuries.

Bladesmithing in the US was bootstrapped into existence by a handful of craftsmen, driven to learn and eager to share their enthusiasm and hard earned knowledge with all others who were attracted to it. Gathering together at hammer-ins, they succeeded in teaching each other through lecture and demonstration. The earliest of these gatherings was held at the field campus of the University of New York at Ashokan. The Ashokan hammer-in or bladesmithing symposium is still an annual event and celebrated its 30 anniversary in 2011.

Alfred Pendray made the trip from Florida to Ashokan with a case of crucibles, iron, and excitement about his work and he shared it all with those who were lucky enough to be present. While his work with wootz was interesting to most, it was Al's new-found metallurgical knowledge gained by working with Dr. Verhoeven that was a benefit to all. Al was the perfect teacher to pass on this new way of looking at what was happening when steel was heated in the fire. He had the practical and intuitive sense of a good smith, but now he shared with us the vocabulary to explain and describe what was taking place. Phase diagrams, time temperature transformation charts, face-centered cubic crystals, and suddenly bladesmithing entered a new level of complexity. Steel became much more than bar stock and the true extent of its mysteries was revealed.

Al Pendray's work with wootz opened the door to history as well. With visions of Assad Allah, the famous Persian smith, watching us forge, bladesmiths of the 20th century became aware of their heritage. With new tools and technology, the new bladesmiths had something to contribute as well. The craft was not just a romantic notion, it was a field of study.

Scholars, scientists, and craftsmen were making new discoveries and their work fed into the new stream of knowledge that was developing around wootz. According to Ann Feuerbach, Hofstra University, Anthropology, "Discussions and experiments on various aspects of crucible Damascus steel production are now often a part of conferences from such diverse fields from material science and blacksmithing to arms collecting, history, archaeology, and anthropology. It is by combining the information from all these diverse disciplines that crucible steel continues to help us understand not only the people and technology of the past, but also the behavior of materials today. It appears that crucible Damascus steel will keep inspiring people in the future." JOM, May 2006

One of the smiths who developed an early interest in steel making was Ric Furrer, Door County Forgeworks, Sturgeon Bay, WI. Ric made his first iron smelt while taking a class from Prof. J. Mark Kenoyer, University of Wisconsin. His dogged research and experimentation has brought him in contact with the leading experts from many disciplines. He demonstrated for the Smithsonian Institution in Washington, DC, in 2002 at the "Silk Road Festival," as well as many hammer-ins and symposiums around the world.

In 2007, Dr. Ann Feuerbach mentioned a conference she was attending at Mehrangarh Fort in Jodhpur, India. It was a study trip and conference on arms and amour covering manufacture and typology as well as current display and care. Curators from the major British museums including the Royal Armories, the British Museum, the Victoria and Albert Museum and the Wallace Collection, joined as the trip was organized by noted scholar, Robert Elgood. When there was a cancellation, Ric Furrer joined the group. They travelled all over North India and examined thousands of old blades held in small museums and private collections of former royal families. Some of the blades were legendary in Indian tradition. Ric said, "This trip was a watershed in my career as a smith and I apply what I learned every time I forge a blade."

# Crucible steelmaking

In the fall of 2010, Ric taught a class on crucible steel making at the New England School of Metalwork, Auburn, Maine. In the class, students were introduced to the history and mystery of crucible steelmaking.

Silicon carbide crucibles were charged with iron powder, carbon, green leaves and green glass. The cap was made from ceramic fiber insulation and sealed with refractory. While the technology differs from the ancient methods, the results are synonymous in both appearance and performance.

The crucible charge was student's choice of pure iron and graphite or pure iron and a specific known chemistry cast iron or iron ore and graphite. Most selected pure iron and cast iron as it is the most controllable/predictable.

Green glass was added along with green plant matter and then the crucible was capped with a piece of ceramic fiber insulation and sealed with high temperature refractory mortar. The crucibles were then fired in a propane furnace and brought

Ric Furrer checking the melt at NESM Crucible Steel Class

Sealing the crucible

Crucible steel class partially filled crucible

Firing the furnace

Checking melt

Removing the crucible after firing

Steel bulat cooling

Dendritic structure visible in cooled bulat

up slowly to 2900 dgerees F or until the charge is fully liquid.

Once the crucibles have reached temperature and soaked for a period, they are checked with a probe for unmelted solids.

Under ideal conditions the furnaces would be shut down and the crucibles allowed to cool slowly, but for purposes of the class, they were removed and allowed to air cool before removing the bulat. Care is taken to not break the crucibles so that they may be reused. There is a layer of glass that needs to be gently chipped away before the crucible will drop free.

When the bulat cooled the dendritic structure of the steel became very apparent.

Once the cakes are cooled they are examined for flaws. Anything that is not solid is ground away. Then it is ready to begin forging. Forging is carefully held to a dull orange heat, not too hot or too cold. According to Ric, "Crucible steel has a rather

Forging the bulat

with very high carbon steel, 1.3 to 2.1% carbon, he proceeded to forge or roll the steel as it cooled from 2200 degrees F. The mechanical action of the forging broke the iron carbide networks as they started to form during cooling. After months of experimentation he found the right combination of mechanical and thermal steps to create steel with ultrafine spherical grains of iron carbide surrounded by grains of ultrafine spherical iron. It was superplastic at high temperatures yet not brittle at room temperature.

The comparison was drawn between his new material, ultrahigh carbon steel, and the ancient Damascus steel. When he looked into the history of Damascus steels, he realized that they contained the same amounts of carbon as his ultrahigh carbon steel. Intrigued, he began working with Jeffrey Wadsworth, Ph.D., to see if they could replicate the surface markings of the old Damascus steel in their new steel.

"First, the ultrahigh carbon steel bar is heated very hot to create coarse iron grains. Second, the bar is cooled very slowly to form a thick continuous network of iron carbide at the boundaries of the coarse iron grains, leaving a continuous network visible to the naked eye. Third, the bar is heated to an intermediate temperature (about 650 to 750 degrees C) and mechanically worked to partially break the network. The network is now no longer continuous (thus, no longer brittle at room temperature) and remains visible as a layered structure, very appealing to the naked eye." (Oleg Sherby R&D Innovator Volume 3, Number 10, October 1994, "Damascus Steel – A Rediscovery?")

In Ric's class there was a wonderful 100% success rate for forging the bulat into bar form. By the end of the process the steel has formed a laminar of carbide and iron. This can be manipulated like a traditional pattern welded blade by incising, forging, to create patterns in the steel.

In California Jeff Pringle has done extensive research into early steel making techniques and has experimented with both crucible and bloomery processes.

narrow forging range, too hot or too cold or too much pressure from the hammer or press and it will fail. When I first started I had about a 50% success rate making the ingots and 50% forging them out....now better than a decade and a half on I do a bit better."

Forging a wootz cake initially is quite surprising, the hammer rebounds off the steel hardly moving it at all. The urge to get it hotter and hit it harder will only make it fall apart, so patience is required for this process. Lots of patience, the pieces were heated and forged forty times before there was any noticeable difference in forgeability. Then as if some stubbornness barrier had been crossed, the wootz cakes began to move. With increasing ease, the cake was coaxed into a bar. Along the way, any cracks or fissures were patiently ground out before continuing to forge.

Forging ultrahigh carbon steel was of interest to Oleg Sherby, Ph.D., Stanford University when he started doing research on superplasticity. Working

Close-up of wootz sword by Ric Furrer

Three wootz sword blades by Ric Furrer

Blade's Guide to Making Knives

Jeff Pringle photo of cooling crucible

Wootz utility knife by Jeff Pringle showing breaking down process of bulat

Wootz sword by
Jeff Pringle

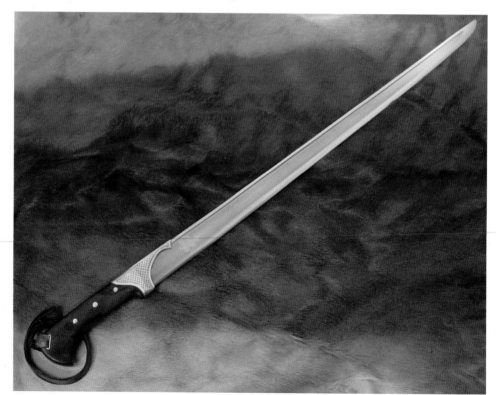

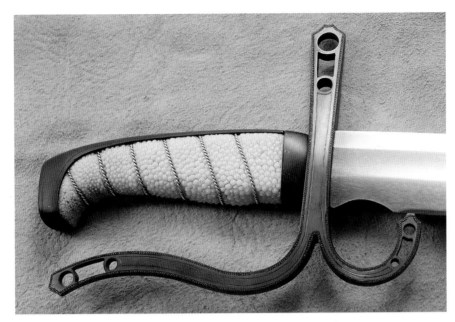

Handle of wootz sword by Jeff Pringle

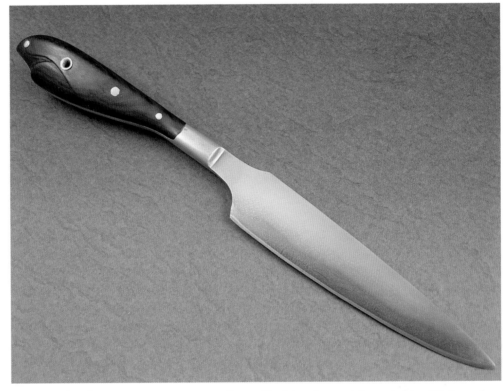

Wootz Integral by Jeff Pringle

Ric Furrer offers classes at his forge, Door County Forgeworks (http://doorcountyforgeworks. com/Welcome.html), and returns for steelmaking classes at New England School of Metalwork (http://www.newenglandschoolofmetalwork.com)

Interest in wootz is popular with makers in Europe and Russia. There is a wealth of information posted on the internet in various forums, including www.bladesmithsforum.com under "Bloomers and Buttons."

Cyrus Haghjoo learned from Achim Wirtz and Andreas Schweikert, Germany. He also studied at the ABS school in Hope, Arkansas.

## Smelting

The other more common method for making steel is by smelting. The use of a furnace to reduce iron ore into steel is common to all Iron Age cultures. From the African ironmasters to the famous Tatara furnace smelt in Japan, this method was the

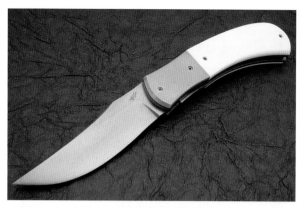

Wootz folding knives by Cyrus Haghjoo

Louis Mills blade polished by John DeMesa

Louis Mills steel close up as polished by John DeMesa
TogiArts.com

most universal way to make steel right up to the introduction of the Bessemer furnace in 1855.

Either hematite ($Fe_2O_3$) or magnetite ($Fe_3O_4$) can be effectively reduced to metallic iron in the right conditions.

- At around 600°F~1500°F $Fe_3O_4 + CO \rightarrow 3FeO + CO_2$
- At around 800°F~1800°F $FeO + CO \rightarrow Fe + CO_2$
- At above 1400°F~1600°F $3Fe + C \rightarrow Fe_3C$

## Louis Mills and a steel forge

For many bladesmiths, it is their interest in Japanese swords that leads them to make their own steel. Louis Mills of Ann Arbor, Michigan, has been making Japanese swords for over 30 years. In an attempt to work closer to the original steels used by the Japanese, he developed a method of making steel in his forge.

Louis made a hand bellows similar to the ones used by Japanese smiths and burned charcoal for fuel in his forge. To make steel, oroshigane, Louis makes a stack of firebrick above his forge bed and then charges the fire with pure iron powder. Pumping air through the bellows and recharging with iron powder and charcoal as the stack burns down, he continues until slag pool at the bottom begins to impinge on the tuyere and limits the air supply from the bellows. When the bricks are cleared a bloom is removed from the forge and hammered flat, quenched and broken into pieces. The pieces are sorted according to carbon content judged by spark testing against a hard wheel grinder. The pieces are then stacked on a paddle and forged welded together, then repeatedly folded and welded until most of the slag and impurities are removed and he has a solid piece of steel from which to forge his blades.

This is perhaps the simplest method I have seen. Its yield is small and, according to Louis, inconsistent, but it is wonderfully accessible.

## The tatara furnace

Traditional Japanese swords are made from tamahagane – the yield of the tatara furnace. The technology is over a thousand years old and came to Japan via Korea and China. It thrived all over Japan as a primary steel making process until modern plants took over in the early 1900s. The destruction and confiscation of Japanese swords after WWII nearly brought the whole tradition to an end. The NBTHK – the Society for the Preservation of Japanese Art Swords – was created to protect and preserve the sword and its production as a cultural heritage. The tatara was rebuilt and in 1977 it was fired again to become the main source of tamahagane for Japanese swordsmiths. It is used to train craftsmen in the production of the steel and recognized as a traditional craft for preservation. The current furnace master is Kihara Akira.

Kihara tapping the slag

Kihara checking the firing, Michael McCarthy is to his left

Examining the kera or bloom with class at University of Minnesota

Sorting the pieces of tamahagane

In June 2004, Professor Wayne Potratz hosted a two week seminar at University of Minnesota Department of Art Sculpture Foundry that featured Akira Kihara. Kihara is designated an "Intangible Cultural Asset" by the Japanese government and is the current murage (furnace master) at the Nittoho Tatara where all the tamahagane is produced.

They built and fired two Kodai Tataras during the two week workshop: one with six tuyeres and a modern tuyere system and one with eight tuyeres and a traditional windbox and pipe system. The yield was in the 75# per burn.

This was a notable event for those interested in smelting and Japanese sword work. Mike Blue, a bladesmith from Minnesota and member of both the Knifemaker's Guild (US) and the Scandinavian Knifemaker's Guild had an active interest in both smelting and crucible steel. I contacted Mike when preparing for this article and he was kind enough to connect me with Prof. Potratz who provided the photographs of that event.

Mike also explained the current theory and chemistry involved with the smelting process. He was careful to note that his explanation was vetted by Alfred Pendray, Dr. John Verhoeven, Daryl Meier, Howard Clark and Akira Kihara. They agreed with his assessment as follows.

At about 1200 degrees F the iron ore becomes hot enough to liberate oxygen from the chemical bond to iron. At this temperature volatiles burn away and slags begin to melt away leaving more surface area for this chemical reaction to take place. If the atmosphere cannot reach the surface of the ore particle, the reaction will not occur."

The reason that powdered iron oxides work better for making steel is that there is a greater surface area on a smaller particle than a large chunk. This justifies roasting native ores and breaking up the larger pieces. It also cleans away some of the preliminary crud that will only clog up the works if left in there.

Calcium carbonates, oyster shell, limestone and granites are used as slag formers. These contribute chemicals that help liquefy the glasses that form and also liberate more carbon dioxides for the atmosphere in the furnace.

The fire is started an allowed to run without iron for up to a couple hours. This drives off any water left in the clay and allows that clay wall to radiate heat back into the system. Operating a furnace is simply containing heat in one place at a hot enough temperature to achieve the work desired. J.E. Rehder in his book, *Mastery and Uses of Fire in Antiquity*," does a good job describing the expected performance of several different furnace configurations.

As the furnace operates longer, the 1200-degree line will rise higher and higher in the stack. The higher 1200-degree line occurs in the furnace, the size of the atmospheric sweet spot increases and this is where the real action, carbon absorption, occurs. We want steel, not simple low carbon

Charging the furnace during firing

irons. Not only that, but using the Japanese model, what is desired is an ultra-high carbon steel at between 1.4-1.6% carbon.

The taller the optimum temperature segment of the stack, the more oxygen is liberated from the iron. This also provides another source of combustion gas to complete the needed chemical reactions, producing a reducing atmosphere where steel will form and begin to coalesce.

When the naked iron is exposed to the burning products of charcoal, carbon dioxide, and in a reducing fire depleted of oxygen above the direct air blast of the tuyeres, the product of incomplete combustion, carbon monoxide, the iron will combine with available carbon and the other burning products will exhaust from the top.

Excess carbon in the form of carbon monoxide and deoxygenated iron are now in a position to form iron carbides and begin the steeling process. The carbon monoxide releases its oxygen and combines with the iron, the released oxygen combines with another CO molecule and forms $CO_2$ and exhausts the stack. The excess carbon combines with the iron.

With higher temperatures this reaction is driven faster. With a taller stack, there is more time to achieve this carbon absorption and diffusion into the iron particles. In several ways this time at temperature equation is the same for pack carburizing. It, too, is a low oxygen carbon rich environment requiring a high enough temperature to start the absorption process and given enough time to achieve a relatively acceptable level of carbon in the new steel. This becomes blister steel which is then folded, etc. to improve diffusion of carbon and is then called shear steel.

Once enough carbon is absorbed, usually considered any value above 2.0% to 4.0% (cast iron), the melting temperature of the iron is lessened to 2100-2200 F and droplets will form hastening the descent of the molten cast iron through the oxygen tuyere zone of the fire. Some carbon will be burned away from the cast iron in the tuyere area, but generally some high carbon steel will remain to fall below the level of the tuyeres into a second reduction zone below the air blast or any slag layers that have formed.

The molten droplets then coalesce into the bloom, self-welding, and if hot enough perhaps even creating a molten puddle of cast steel.

Removing the bloom, forging into plates or coins, sorting, stacking and welding all are part of the process of removing the remaining crud (slag glasses, sand, clay, charcoal, dirt, etc.) and homogenizing the steel. The entire "mystery" of folding and welding steel is nothing more than cleaning the steel bloom of any remaining slag, sand, clay, charcoal or open spaces to form a homogenous bar of usable steel. The number of folds and welds also gives the carbon an opportunity to diffuse evenly throughout the billet.

It's a lot of work. Three days to build the stack is the shortest ideal time for drying the clay walls. Humidity will make running the fire that much more difficult. One day to burn and several days to coalesce the bloom. For a blade, the smith then selects good material for the edge, lesser quality for the spine. This requires likely several burns to achieve an adequate supply to choose from. Lifetimes in the case of Japanese smiths, who often receive tamahagane from their grandfather's collections and begin saving portions of good material for their grandsons.

There is no reason not to recycle poorly developed steel that did not have enough atmosphere exposure, too little surface area or too little time at temperature, but it's a second or third burn and that much more work. Slags can also be recycled to recover iron lost to those glasses. Recovering slag is the basis for the Toledo steel legend. As their refining processes improved, there were large numbers of ready, easy to gather, iron rich, Roman slag pits all over that region of Spain.

Mike followed up his class with Kihara by accepting his invitation to participate in the tatara firing in Japan. Since then Mike has done many smelts on his own and at various bladesmith gatherings. He was invited to England to participate in a smelt at Jack Hobson's forge in Kent, England and has returned numerous times.

## The Catalan forge

There are many different versions of the backyard smelter and one of the more historically famous is the Catalan forge from Spain. Dr. Jesus Hernandez (http://www.jhbladesmith.com) was attracted to the Japanese sword and its mysticism. He practiced Japanese-style fencing and his teachers introduced him to the appreciation of the Japanese sword.

When Jesus started to make swords, it became apparent that, for him to capture all the nuance of grain and hamon, he was going to have to learn to make his own steel. "The interaction of the hada

On left, Mike Blue and "Doc" Price building furnace, Jack Hobson is peeking out from behind.

and the hamon is responsible for creating a complex number of different visual activities (hataraki) in the steel. When this steel is skillfully polished, all these beautiful details become visible to the naked eye," he said.

He built a number of bloomery furnaces in the style of the Japanese tatara, Kodai tatara, but after meeting with a fellow bladesmith from Barcelona, he became interested in the Catalan forge of his own Spanish traditions. The Catalan forge was introduced around 700AD and the design was refined and in use right up the 1800s. The most striking difference in the Catalan forge is that the charge is separated by a dividing wall, so the fine ore is charged near the tuyere and the coarse ore in the other half.

The main reduction takes place in the part filled with the coarse ore through which the hot gases pass. The fine ore is responsible for establishing a FeO-rich slag bath, which refines the carbon rich metal. The quality of the metal is controlled by the character of the slag. This makes a unique reduction and refining process at the same time. In the bloomery process, a second step is needed to refine the metal.

The rough iron ore was picked up as scale from previous forging operations and used for this smelt to challenge the process. If steel could be made with this material then better ore would be a predictably better end product.

Tanto by Jesus Hernandez

Design of Catalan forge by Jesus Hernandez

Charged Catalan showing divider

The divider is removed for the burn down

Pulverizing roasted ore

The furnace is recharged during burn

Firing the Catalan

Burning down the Catalan

The resulting bloom from Catalan

Bloom broken down into bars

Consolidated billet after folding and welding

Stack of bars ready to be rewelded

Billet rough ground and etched to see grain

Heating stack in welding forge

Casting firebrick for furnace

Jesus Hernandez folding and welding billet

The iron ore was gathered locally, roasted and then pulverized with a hammer to make it much finer.

The fire is started and charged as it burns. Within a half hour of starting the burn, the temperature in ore chamber reached 1500 degrees F.

The fire is continually charged at about 500g of ore and 1kg of charcoal keeping the ore near the further wall away from the tuyere.

Another advantage to this furnace is that it is reusable. The bricks were cast from fire clay, vermiculite, ash, and sand. Casting the brick reduces the expense. There are more pictures and information at Jesus Hernandez Bladesmith (http://www.jhbladesmith.com).

Once the bloom is made, it has to be flattened and consolidated. The bloom is filled with slag and inclusions at this point and feels quite spongy under the hammer. It welds to itself easily without flux because of the slag and needs to be folded and welded many times before it begins to stiffen into solid steel. Whether the bloom is flattened into pieces and restacked or consolidated into bars and stacked, the process is the same.

## Kodai-type furnaces

Jesus also builds Kodai-type furnaces and begins by casting his own firebrick made from fireclay, vermiculite, ash and sand.

The air supply is connected using iron pipe fittings.

The plug in the T can be removed to use as a peep hole into the fire. The end of the tuyere or air

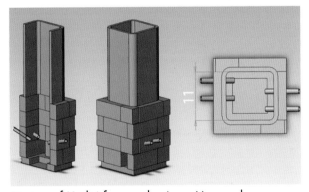

Design of Kodai furnace by Jesus Hernandez

Constructed base for furnace with air supply

Looking through the peep hole into furnace

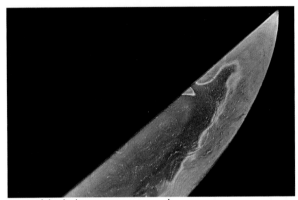

Tanto blade by Jesus Hernandez

pipe that protrudes into the furnace will melt and is disposable. Copper and ceramic tuyere tips have been made to last longer.

Heat treated and polished, the blade shows the character of the steel that Jesus Hernandez was looking for when he began his work.

## Smelting resources

Other artists have taken an interest in smelting as well. Inspired by accounts of African iron smelting, Lee Sauder and Skip Williams (http://iron.wlu.edu) began experimenting with small scale smelting in 1999. After participating in Early Iron Symposium in 2004 at the Farmer's Museum, Cooperstown, NY, they shared their knowledge with other enthusiasts, Darrell Markewitz http://www.warehamforge.ca/ironsmelting/index.html and Michael McCarthy of the Farmer's Museum and formed an early iron smelters group, publishing their research online. Their contributions via classes and demonstrations, as well as generous internet postings, coalesced with bladesmiths

Lee Sauder's
Nyamakala Gash

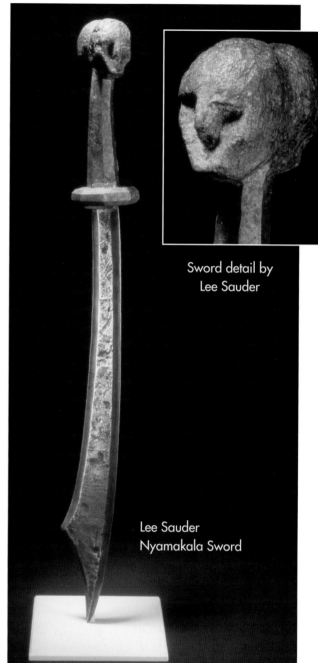

Sword detail by
Lee Sauder

Lee Sauder
Nyamakala Sword

experimenting on their own. The open sharing of information, sources, and often labor at various public smelts held around the country, helped to expand everyone's knowledge immensely.

Lee uses his material for sculpture and iron work. Making his own iron allows his to explore the material in way not possible with bar stock.

Interest in this archaic craft has become a worldwide phenomenon. Smiths in England, Europe, Russia, Scandinavia, Czech Republic, India, Japan, Africa, all over the world, are connecting via the internet and symposiums. It is community of smiths who share a similar passion for iron making, and when they gather around the fire it unites us all.

Doing research is expensive and sharing hard earned knowledge is extremely generous, but time and time again we find the openness and generosity of smiths unselfishly given. Their enthusiasm is infectious and their genuine curiosity stimulating. We share a long history in the fire, it is part of what makes us human and certainly the modern smiths are teaching by example what being human truly means.

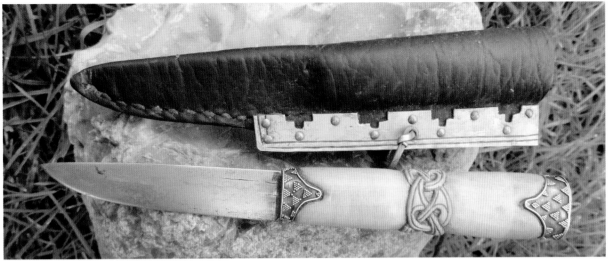

Petr Floriánek Viking utility (petr.florianek@seznam.cz), inspired by Patrick Barta (http://templ.net/english/weapons-antiquity_and_early_middle_age.php)

VikingSaex by Petr Floriánek Czech Republic

Don Fogg
98 Lake St.
Auburn, Maine 04210

The author extends special thanks to:
Alfred Pendray, Williston, FL
Dr. J. D. Verhoeven, metallurgist
 Iowa State University
Ric Furrer, Sturgeon Bay, WI
Mike Blue, Canon Falls, MN
Jeff Pringle, Oakland, CA
Jesus Hernandez, Roanoke, VA
Wayne Potratz, University of Minnesota
John DeMesa, Lewisville, TX
Petr Floriánek, Czech Republic
Owen Bush, Kent, England
Mick Maxen, England
Cyrus Haghjoo, Solingen, Germany

Big stack by Mick Maxen, England

# Making and Carving a Scottish Dirk

## by Vince & Grace Evans

The 18th-century Scottish dirk with its interlace carved wooden grip is a recognizable knife often worn today with traditional Scottish attire. Although many traditional dirk grips were ornately carved, they served for everyday use and carry. It is a misconception that the common man's dirk was plain and unembellished.

Although the grips vary, in our research of historic pieces we discovered an overwhelming majority of carved dirks. Some of the carving was less refined, but at least one form of carving was invariably present. A few exceptions include dirk grips of pewter, brass, horn and ivory, but even then, many of those were embellished or decorated.

Original dirk grips are found in a variety of shapes and sizes. Typical grips range from four to 4-3/8 inches, with some 4-1/2 inches or longer, and others shorter than four inches. Generally, antique knives and swords are much more petite in proportion than people realize today. Sheaths were either wet-formed leather or leather over a wooden core, some with pockets in the front for a knife and fork. Handle and sheath fittings were brass, silver, and occasionally, iron.

Blades were often fashioned from cut-down swords, thus fullers are common. The spine thicknesses vary from about 3/16 inch up to 1/2 inch. We discovered dirks with double-edged blades and a few featuring slightly curved blades. They tend to show obvious markings of having formerly been sword blades, with the telltale signs usually in the form of German smiths' hallmarks. The blades

Research is an important part of recreating an antique sword or knife. Here Vince and Grace Evans examine an antique Scottish dirk made by John MacLeod of Edinburgh.

forged specifically for dirks are single edged, tapering from spine to edge, and hilt to point. Filework decorates the spine of the occasional early blade, but it became a more common embellishment in the 19th century.

For this project, we are making a dirk with a single-edged blade and a four-inch grip. The blade will have a single, narrow fuller and will not be fileworked. If you are not ready to make your own blade, there are several retailers who sell non-mounted, completed Scottish dirk blades that you can craft a handle for using our methods.

The following lists show the materials, tools and equipment that were used in the making of this dirk. Many of my tools are handmade for the task at hand. These exact tools and materials are not necessary for the crafting of a dirk.

## Materials

10 x 1-1/2 x 1/4-inch piece of 5160 tool steel
Walnut block 4-1/4 x 2 x 2 inches
1/32-inch (20 gauge) brass sheet for fittings
5/16 inch brass rod for ball end
1/8-inch brass rod for suspension loop
Sandpaper: 320 and 600 grit
High-temperature silver solder and corresponding flux
Basswood for sheath
Tung Oil
Bookbinder's leather
Contact cement
Epoxy
Cold bluing solution
Layout ink (i.e. Dykem)

## Hand Tools & Equipment

Drill press and bits (size will depend on tang dimension)
Assorted files: jeweler's files, flat and pillar files
Assorted chisels: 1/16 to 3/16 inch wide for interlace, 3/8 to one inch for sheath work
Steel scribe
Razor saw
Jeweler's saw
Propane torch
Assorted small hammers

Sanding block
Sharp hobby knife
Hand planes
Checkering file
Line gravers
Belt grinder
Disk sander
Lathe

## Forging and blade dimensions

I started with a 10 x 1-1/2 x 1/4-inch piece of 5160 tool steel. My first step is to forge the long, narrow tang, tapering down to approximately 1/4-inch round. This end will later be threaded. The remaining steel is forged into a long triangular blade profile, tapering in cross section both from hilt to point and from spine to edge. I start by forging the tang first so that whatever remaining steel I have left will become the blade, especially since I don't have a specific blade length in mind, just a

Forging the tang.

Forging the point.

general idea. It takes the guesswork out how much leftover steel is needed for the tang. Once the forging is completed and I am satisfied with the shape, the blade is brought up to cherry red and annealed in vermiculite.

## Grinding the blade

Once the blade has cooled down, check it for straightness. If there are any warps, you will need to correct these before you begin grinding your blade. A properly annealed blade should straighten easily in a vise. Sometimes the jaws of a heavy wrench can be used for leverage.

When grinding blades, be sure to wear a respirator, safety glasses and head covering. I also wear thick leather gloves when doing heavy grinding to protect my hands from heat and the grinding belt.

The rough-forged blank is first de-scaled with a stone grinder. I use a 4-1/2-inch right-angle grinder with the blade clamped to my anvil. Forge scale will dull normal grinding belts and files. The de-barked blade is then shaped on a 2 x 72-inch belt grinder, following the general lines and dimensions that were forged. Dirk blades typically do not have a ricasso or thickened area near the hilt, so the triangular blade cross section goes all the way into the tang. The general grinding is done on a 60-grit belt followed by a 120-grit belt. I flat grind on the platen of my belt grinder to maintain an even face on the blade. Flat grinding may take some practice if you are used to working on a contact wheel.

To get an even grind on the face of the blade, be sure to use sharp belts. A notched piece of wood or a tool holder will help in holding the blade when grinding on the platen. Leave the edge of the blade 1/16-inch thick before heat-treating to lessen the possibility of warping. After heat-treating, you can grind the blade on a 220-grit belt to thin the edge down. If you do not have a belt grinder, an alternative to shaping the blade is to use a draw file.

A false edge is ground in the lower third of the spine of the blade, the bevel being 3/16 to 1/4 inch wide and tapering towards the point.

This blade has a narrow fuller near the spine so the next step is scraping in the fuller using a

Grinding the blade profile.

Grinding the blade flats.

straight edge and round scrapers. Since many original dirk blades were made from cut down swords, the fuller runs the entire length of the blade and tapers off as it comes to the point. The straight edge guide can be a thick piece of flat bar clamped to the blade. My round scrapers are made from chainsaw files with the ends ground square and sharp.

Simply push the scraper down the blade against your flat bar. The steady, repetitive push will quickly start a groove in the surface of the blade. I once witnessed this being demonstrated by a Japanese blade smith and it impressed me at how quickly he was able to scrape in the fuller. I do not use any lubricant in my scraping as I found that it tends to cause a hard skin on the blade that is difficult to remove. You may also use a small-diameter contact wheel for a wider fuller if you have one for your belt grinder.

Scraping the fuller into the blade.

Cleaning up the fuller with sandpaper and sanding block.

Polishing the blade.

Once the desired depth of the fuller is reached, all scraper marks must be sanded out prior to heat-treating. This is done using sandpaper wrapped around a Micarta® sanding block with a radius that matches the fuller. Typically 120-grit sandpaper takes out the scraper marks, and then the fuller is polished to a 220-grit finish. An alternative is to use small EDM stones for the polishing of the fuller.

The end of the tang is threaded. The size will depend on the overall thickness of the finished blade and tang. This blade has a 10-24 thread. You will need to thread the last inch or so of the tang, depending on how much excess protrudes from the pommel end. Be sure to leave enough thread exposed for your tang nut.

The blade is heat-treated to a hard spring temper by heating the entire blade to critical temperature (1,450 degrees F) and quenching it in oil, then drawing to a vermillion color (bronze into purple). The blade can be put in an oven at 425 degrees F for an hour. This should give the correct color and hardness. The heat-treated blade is now hand polished using 220- and 400-grit wet or dry sandpaper and a flat sanding block. During this polishing process I sometimes use a diamond lapping plate to bring the flat of the blade down into the cutting edge. Be sure to also polish the fuller to a 400-grit finish.

If you use a belt grinder for your grinding work, a friend taught me to use old J-Flex belts for the hand polishing process. The 220-grit belts that may have seemed dull on your grinder are really quite sharp when used by hand on a sanding block. This method works with belts from 120 grit and finer.

Now that you've finished your blade, make a sleeve out of paper, not only to protect it, but to also protect yourself from the edge. The next step will make your dirk distinctive and personal.

# Dimensions and layout of the grip

A block of walnut 4-1/4 x 2 x 2 inches was chosen for this project. Although there has been much discussion as to the types of wood used on original dirk grips, the ones we observed were typically reddish-brown and tight grained, many times with a burly look to them, possibly heath root. We have also seen oak, maple and walnut, along with a few other types of wood. Walnut is a good choice

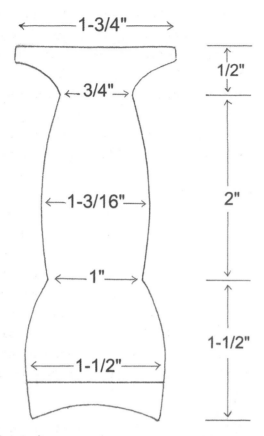

Dirk grip dimensions.

Drilling the pilot hole in the grip.

for beginner projects in carving dirk grips as it is easily carved, and holds detail well. We have used different types of briarwood, which has a burled appearance similar to originals but is more difficult to carve.

For descriptive purposes, we will divide the grip into three sections: the haunch (the lower portion of the grip), the barrel (the center portion) and the pommel. The template shown will give you dimensions for the grip used in this project. The haunch width can vary depending on the finished width of

Turning the grip's profile on the lathe.

Marking the tang width.

your blade, but is usually 1/4 inch wider than your blade.

Since the grip is initially turned on a lathe, a pilot hole is drilled through it that will eventually be the pilot hole for the tang. To find the center of your block, draw lines from corner to corner on both ends of your block. The points where your lines cross should be the center of your block. This hole is best drilled on a drill press. The general profile shape is turned on a lathe and smoothed out with sandpaper. Because I have a lathe, I use it to help maintain a uniform profile of the grip shape. The grip could also be shaped freehand using coarse files or a belt grinder.

Many original grips have an arch where the blade meets the handle, so a radius is ground into the end of the grip where it will eventually converge with the steel. For this project I used a five-inch-diameter contact wheel. A matching radius was also filed on the base of the blade. The width of the tang base is marked on the end of the grip and small pilot holes drilled.

A narrow flat file is used to connect the holes and enlarge the slot to fit the tang. The tang can

Filing the tang hole.

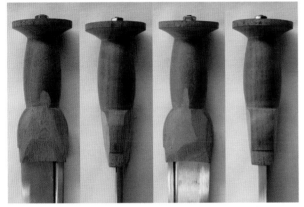

The excess wood is removed from the lower front and back of the grip.

Refining the haunches and lower point of the grip.

The barrel of the grip is filed to a slight oval.

also be heated and burned into the slot for a final fit. Be sure to remove the hot tang once it is seated or you could over-burn the hole, and heat can also cause the wood to crack. If your blade is already heat-treated, be sure not to overheat the base of the blade or you could remove some of its temper. It is acceptable for the tang not to be tempered.

Once you have fitted your blade to your rough-turned grip you can begin to shape the cross section of your grip. Be sure to secure your blade to your grip with a temporary nut on the pommel end. I use a combination of a belt grinder, files and chisels for shaping the wood. You will notice in the accompanying side-view picture that the haunches are flat, kind of like wings. Use a file to cut down the wood until the flat of the haunches extends beyond the blade by about 3/16 inch. A razor saw was used to cut a line around the base of the grip about 5/8" from the end. This will become the recess for your metal ferrule. The excess wood is cut away with a chisel.

To help me remember which side I am working on, I mark the front of the grip and the top of the pommel with an "F." This also helps when assembling the grip as I usually keep all solder joints to the back of the grip, the side that would be against the body when worn.

Using chisels and files extend the line of the barrel into a rounded point on the face of the haunch. The faces of the barrel are flattened to create an oval cross section. When the shaping is complete, sand all surfaces smooth.

A ferrule, or metal collar, at the base of the grip keeps the wood from splitting in use and was typical on Scottish dirks from about 1700 forward. Many earlier dirks do not have ferrules or pommel caps and tend to be missing portions of their grips today. To make our ferrule, we start with a template of half of the ferrule made of thin cardboard. Cereal-box-type cardboard works well as template material because it is similar in thickness to the brass sheet we are using. Two halves are traced onto a 1/32-inch brass sheet that has been coated with blue layout ink. The pieces are cut out and lightly hammered to fit the curvature of the grip.

A cardboard template of the ferrule is made.

Test fitting one side of the ferrule.

The ferrule pieces are hammered to fit the curvature of the wood.

The faceplate is drilled and filed to fit over the tang.

This can be done over the edge of a small anvil or a small-diameter steel rod clamped in a vise.

Test fit the piece periodically while shaping it to get a good fit. Depending on the condition of your brass material, it may have to be annealed to work easily under the hammer. If you cannot bend the brass between your fingers with little effort, you must anneal it to prevent work hardening and make your shaping job easier. To anneal the brass, heat it with a propane torch to a dull glow and quench in water. The two shaped halves are now fluxed and soldered together using a high-temperature silver solder.

The oxidized and soldered piece is cleaned through pickling in a phosphoric acid bath. This is nothing more than driveway and concrete cleaner that can be found at a hardware store. After the brass is cleaned, rinse it in a baking soda solution or under running water to neutralize the acid. The assembled ferrule is test fitted to the end of the

The faceplate is scribed to line up with the grip in place.

grip. You may need to file some wood away or tap the fitting lightly with a small hammer to get a snug fit. Sand or file any excess metal down flush to the wood on the end of the grip.

To make a faceplate for your ferrule, cut a piece of brass a little longer and a little wider than your ferrule. The plate is marked for center and measured for a hole to match the base of the tang. It is then drilled and cut out with a jeweler's saw to fit over the tang. The faceplate is tapped with a hammer to fit the curvature of the ferrule and scribed to line up with the grip in place. The ferrule is lined up on the faceplate and soldered to it. The excess brass is trimmed off and the solder cleaned up.

Test fit your blade to the grip with the ferrule in place. Make any final adjustments with a small file so everything fits together well. The base of your blade should fit flush to the faceplate with no gaps. You may need to file the shoulders of your blade to get a good seat against the faceplate. Be sure to clean up any excess solder with small files and sandpaper or the solder will show as silver spots on your brass fittings.

There are many patterns of interlace. This dirk is one of the simpler patterns to carve. It will include two rows of interlace on the barrel, plus a trefoil and a crossover loop on each side of the haunch. When laying out your interlace pattern, make sure to draw your rows butted up against each other. This will give your interlace a tighter appearance when carved.

It is confusing to describe the layout process in words, so it might be helpful to refer to the accompanying photos for a visual description. You will be using a pencil and eraser for laying out the pattern. Starting 1/4" above the top of the haunches, draw a line around the barrel of the grip. Draw another line halfway between the bottom of the pommel and your first line. You should now have

a barrel divided into two equal sections. For each row of interlace, start by drawing four arches, upper and lower, equally spaced. The lower arches sit halfway between and opposing the upper ones. These will become the upper and lower curves of your interlace.

Starting at one of the upper arches, connect each interlacing band by drawing a connecting band to the lower arch that sits two spaces over. You will then continue this band up to the arch that is just behind the arch you started from. Continue connecting your interlace band using this sequence until it is complete. You will need to erase the excess lines where two bands overlap to begin the over/under pattern. When you are done laying out a row, you should have one continuous, never-ending band. You will know if you have not laid out your interlace correctly as you will not end up with a continuous single band. If you are not sure how to layout the interlace pattern, you can practice on a wooden dowel of similar diameter to your grip before laying it out on your actual grip.

Once you have two bands of interlace drawn around your barrel, your next step is to pattern or design the trefoil on the lower point of your grip. The trefoil is a common interlace pattern seen on Celtic artwork. This is simply a three-pointed knot pattern. A crossover band with loops on the face of each haunch completes the hilt design.

Starting to draw the interlace pattern on the grip.

Interlace pattern laid out.

Rotating vise made by George Gibo.

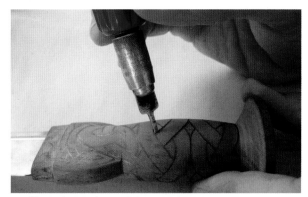

Profiling the outline of the interlace.

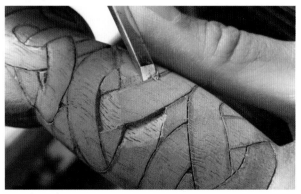

Beveling the junctions.

## Rotating vice

One piece of equipment that I use on an almost daily basis is a rotating vise that was made for me by my friend and fellow knifemaker, George Gibo. This vise allows me to rotate a piece for ease of access to all sides of the handle that I am working on. The basic construction is made up of two pieces of pipe, one that fits snugly inside the other with just enough clearance to rotate. The outer pipe has a tightening bolt to secure the inner pipe in set positions. The inner pipe protrudes about two inches from the outer pipe to allow for a tightening bolt that presses against the wooden liners. A blade may be clamped securely within the wooden liner, with the grip exposed for carving. This versatile piece of equipment with an inner diameter pipe measurement of two inches has been used for work on the majority of my pieces, including swords.

## Carving

The outline of the interlace pattern is profiled by cutting along the lines with a thin, narrow chisel. You could also use a sharp hobby knife. The junctions are beveled to create the over/under appearance. Begin by carving a chip out where the band appears to pass under another band. How deeply you carve your grip will depend on personal preference. We have seen shallow and deep carving on original dirk grips. Continue carving until all junctions have been beveled on the row you are working on. Once you have established where the junctions are, you are now ready to start the actual carving of the bands.

The edges of the bands are carved away to create the rounded appearance of woven cord or leather. Your bands should not have gaps between them. The grain of the wood may change direction, which will affect the direction in which you carve. If you encounter resistance or chipping of the wood, try carving from the opposite direction. Keeping your chisels extremely sharp will help avoid chipping and give you a smoother finish.

When you have finished carving your first band, repeat the same steps for the second row. When you have completed carving both rows, carve away the excess wood where the base of the pommel meets the upper row of interlace. These little details are what will give your interlace depth.

The sharp edges of the knobs where the pattern intersects are carved away to create smooth domes. A sharp-pointed hobby knife will help in this process. Not all dirks had these knobs at the intersections. You can choose to layout your interlace pattern with or without these knobs. In Georgian- and Victorian-era dirks, these carved wooden knobs evolved into silver or brass pins and the interlace pattern of the classic 18th-century

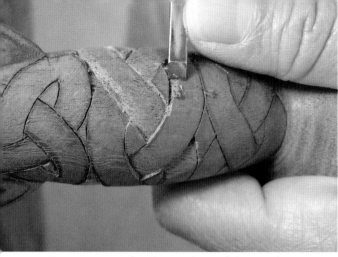

Carving away the sharp edges of the interlace.

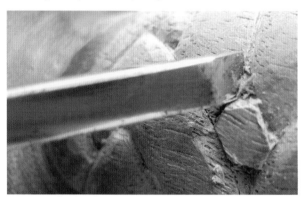

Carving the knobs.

Rough carved knob.

Carving the crossover.

Carving away the excess wood to make the interlace stand proud.

dirk became a simpler diamond-shaped, basket-weave pattern.

The trefoil will carve the same way as the interlace bands. Start first by profiling the pattern along the lines you have drawn, keeping in mind that the top of your trefoil should be tight against your lower row of interlace. Again, bevel the junctions where the bands meet to create the over/under appearance. Carve away the edges of the trefoil to create the rounded effect. You will notice that the trefoil appears to stand above the lower point of the barrel.

Sanding the grip with 320-grit sandpaper.

Making and Carving a Scottish Dirk

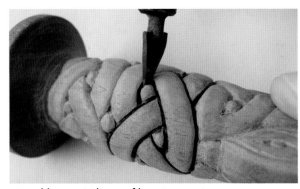

Wood burning the profile.

Wood burning in the accent lines.

After profiling the crossover design, the sharp edges of the band are removed. The excess wood on the haunches around the crossover design are carved away to make the interlace stand proud.

Once the grip is carved, it is sanded with 320-grit sandpaper wrapped around a wedge-shaped Micarta™ sanding block to remove sharp edges and chisel marks.

## Detailing

Most original dirks had fine lines along the bands of their interlace carving. Over time, many of these fine lines have worn smooth but can still be seen at the junctions. We use a wood-burning tool to create the lines on our dirks. Wood burning is not necessary but we include it to help define the interlace pattern. A chisel, scraper, sharp knife or three-cornered file could also be used to cut in your lines. The wood-burning tool that I use is a simple hobby shop model that I made a custom tip for out of a piece of heavy brass sheet. It is basically a thin knife-like point that allows us to get into the tighter portions of the interlace pattern.

First we burn the profile of the interlace pattern, then go back and burn in lines on the face of the bands to give definition to the carving. We find it easiest to start burning the centerline on the band and then burn in lines that are parallel to that centerline.

Many original dirks have carved decorations on the underside of the pommels. These can range from more interlace carving and fluting to various layered leaf-like patterns. The underside of the pommel on this project is laid out with a simple leaf pattern. I divide the underside of the pommel into eight even sections. Each of these lines will be the center vein of a leaf. I then draw curved lines on either side of the vein to create a leaf appearance. Once all eight leaves are drawn, I then draw lines out from where two leaves come together to create what looks like an under layer of leaves. When you are done, you should have 16 leaves under your pommel, eight large outer-layer leaves and eight smaller under-layer leaves.

The lines of these leaves are then profiled. The next step is to carve the vein of each of the eight large leaves. You are cutting the end grain of the wood so it will actually be scraping the wood away with your chisel edge. Put one corner of your chisel in the vein line at a slight angle and gently push from the outer rim of the pommel toward the barrel of your grip. When you have done both sides of the vein line, your leaf should have a "V" cleft down the middle. Repeat this step for all the leaves in the upper layer.

The lower layer of leaves is carved in the same manner except that you need to relieve the wood at the point where the lower leaf tucks under the upper layer. Again, this detail adds depth to your carving. The final rim of wood around the leaf tips should be carved away.

Sand the carving under the pommel with 320-grit sandpaper and wood-burn the profile design. After all of the carving and wood burning is complete, we again lightly sand the grip with fine sandpaper to smooth out any burrs raised by the wood burning.

Carving under the pommel.

Wood burning under the pommel.

# Hilt fittings

Many original dirks had metal side straps running along the edges of the haunches. Some grips were left plain and some had the edges of the haunches decoratively carved. For this project we will attach narrow side straps made out of brass to match the other fittings. First, a channel is carved into the wood for the side straps. Typically the edge of the haunch on the cutting edge side is narrower than the spine side so your side straps will

Relieving panel for side strap.

Brass side strap.

Drilling hole for strap pin.

A narrow strip of brass is wrapped for pommel ring.

Side strap tucked under ferrule.

Accent lines are cut in with a Barrett file.

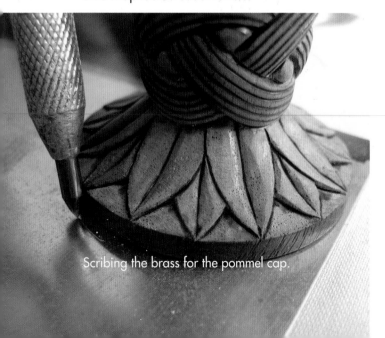

Scribing the brass for the pommel cap.

The pommel cap design is cut in with a graver.

be different widths. A brass strip is cut and filed to fit each channel. The strips will need to be curved to fit the curvature of the haunch by hammering over a small anvil. Test-fit your side straps and make adjustments to either the brass or the wood until each fits snugly and is flush with the surface of the wood.

Pinholes are drilled at the top of each side strap and the lower ends are notched with a file to fit under the edge of the ferrule. Not all original side straps have pins holding them in place. You could also notch into the wood on the top end of the haunch so that the end of your side strap tucks into that notch and is held in when the ferrule is fitted in place.

The pommel cap is made from a narrow strip and a flat disk cut from sheet brass. Measure the strip by wrapping a strip of cardboard around the pommel rim and marking the length. Transfer this measurement to a piece of sheet brass coated with blue layout ink. The width of your brass strip will depend on the thickness of the wood of your pommel. Cut out and anneal your brass strip. The strip is then formed by hand around the wooden pommel and soldered together.

When the ring is soldered and the joint filed smooth, test-fit it to the pommel and make any adjustments to the roundness so that it sits snugly and evenly to the rim of your pommel. Trace the shape of your pommel onto your brass sheet, making sure to allow enough extra for the brass ring to fit. The disk is cut out and tapped flat so that it has no high spots. Your brass ring is then soldered to the disk. The excess brass is trimmed off and sanded smooth.

The pommel edge is dressed and a hole is drilled in the center of the pommel cap for the tang. Accent lines are scribed on the edge of the pommel and the ferrule, and cut in with a Barrette file, then sanded clean. The pommel cap of original dirks was one place that was often decorated. It could have been as simple as a series of concentric circles or even pierced with various designs such as hearts. Occasionally you would even find a coin used as a pommel cap.

For this project a common compass pattern is drawn on the face of the pommel cap. This is laid out in a similar manner to the leaves that we did under the pommel. We first scribe a series of circles, one near the outer rim and one around the center hole, leaving approximately 1/4 inch distance to the hole. The face of the cap is divided into eight equal sections and lines drawn to create an eight-pointed star. These lines are cut in with a line graver. Half of each star point is shaded with a series of fine lines to accent the design. Once the hilt fittings have all been accented or engraved, I wet sand all fittings with 400-grit sandpaper.

Now that you are done with most of the handling of your grip, several coats of tung oil are applied to seal the grip and allowed to cure for several days.

## Sheath

Most historical dirk sheaths were leather that was wet-formed to fit over the blade. Occasionally, wood-lined sheaths were used and became more common in later years. We prefer using a wood-lined sheath for its longevity and durability. The walls of our sheaths are kept thin to give the appearance of an all-leather sheath.

I prefer to use basswood, but a similar wood such as alder could be used for the sheath. Avoid using woods such as oak that tend to be acidic and could cause a rust problem on your blade. We will be using chisels and block planes to do the carving and shaping of our sheath. I don't recommend using sandpaper for any of the work on what will be

Basswood laid out for sheath.

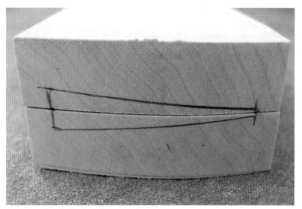

Profile for blade channel.

Carving away excess wood.

One side of the sheath is carved.

the inside of your sheath because sandpaper grit could lodge in the wood and scratch your blade.

We will begin by tracing the blade onto two 1/2-inch-thick pieces of wood, leaving approximately 3/16 inch border of wood around the profile of the blade. Be sure to trace one left- and one right-side profile. Put a mark on the wood to indicate which side of the blade profile is your cutting edge. Cut out your wood pieces with a saw following the outer line. The throat end of the wood will need to be shaped to fit the curvature of the base of your grip where it sits against the ferrule. This can be done with a file or a sander.

Using a sharp knife, cut into the wood along the profile line that you drew around the dirk blade. Clamp your two pieces of wood together and draw lines to indicate the thickness and taper of your blade cross section. This will become the mouth opening of your sheath. The mouth of the sheath is carved to establish channel depth by cutting along the lines you drew on the end of the wood. You will now begin to carve away the channel for the blade.

When our sheath is carved out, the only portion of the blade that touches the wood is the base and the very tip. Placing your wood on a flat surface and using a gouge-type chisel, begin carving the excess wood away. Remember that you are only carving a channel as deep as half the thickness of your blade from each side of your sheath. The spine side of the blade channel should be much deeper than the edge side of your channel.

Periodically lay your blade in the channel to check for fit. When it sits nicely in the channel and

is half sunken into the wood, carve the other side of the sheath to match. When you feel both sides are carved to fit, clamp them together and attempt to slip your blade into the opening. Do this several times. Depending on if your blade is tight or loose will determine what your next step is. If your blade is tight, unclamp your pieces and look at your channels to see if your blade has left dark rub spots on the wood. These high spots will need to be shaved down for a proper fit. If your blade is not leaving dark spots, you can scribble some pencil lines on your blade faces and on the spine and then do a test fit.

The pencil marks should now leave dark spots on your wood, which will indicate the high spots on your channel to be shaved down. Continue these steps until you get a nice fit with no dark rub spots. The fit should be snug when the last 1/2 inch or so of the blade is pushed into the sheath. If your problem is that the sheath is too loose after you carve it and clamp it together for a test fit, it means that your channel is cut too deep. To correct this problem, take each half of your sheath

Trace profile without ferrule.

Planing the sheath profile.

Relieving the wood where the leather tucks under the fitting.

and lay it channel down on a piece of 220-grit sandpaper on a hard, flat surface. Gently rub it back and forth to take off some of the excess wood. Check periodically for fit by clamping the pieces back together and test fitting your blade.

Once both halves of the sheath are carved out and the blade fits snugly in the clamped pieces, they are ready to be glued together. Run a narrow bead of carpenter's glue along the edges of one side of your sheath and clamp it to the other side, making sure that the mouth opening lines up

correctly. Test-fit your blade in the clamped, glued sheath and make any adjustments by loosening the clamps and lining everything up so that the blade fits nicely. Remove the blade from the sheath and wash any glue off of the blade that may have stuck to it.

When the glued sheath is cured, place the blade, with grip attached, in the sheath. We do this to determine the final outer shape and thickness of the sheath. A profile line is drawn on the mouth of the sheath around the base of the grip without the ferrule in place. The wood of the sheath is then planed down to the profile line that was drawn onto the mouth of the sheath. This will ensure that your sheath and grip area transition smoothly. Your sheath should not stick out farther than the base of your grip. The sheath should taper in thickness from hilt to point and from spine to edge. When you are satisfied with the final shape, lightly sand the entire outside of the sheath to remove any irregularities or plane marks.

Many original dirk sheaths had designs tooled into the leather on the face of the sheath. Because our sheath has a wooden core, the design is laid out on the wood and cut in with a checkering file. You could also burn the design in deeply with a wood-burning tool. A common design was a series of "X's" drawn on the face of the sheath. We will be using thin bookbinder's leather that will be glued and tooled into the design in the wood.

The wood is relieved where the leather will tuck under the brass throat piece. Do this by scoring a line around the sheath with a sharp knife, approximately 1/2 inch below the throat. The wood is carved or filed away below the cut line to the depth of your leather thickness. This cut can taper back into the body of your sheath.

## Sheath fittings

When I make a throat piece, I typically put my solder joint down the back center of the fitting. The tip fitting (chape) is made from two halves, front and back, with solder joints on either edge. Cardboard templates are made for the throat and tip pieces and scribed onto a brass sheet that has been coated with blue layout ink. The pieces are cut out and annealed. The throat piece is formed over a steel rod to roughly the same shape as the cross section of the sheath. The rough-formed fitting is tapped to fit snugly over the wood with the blade in place to prevent cracking the wood.

When the throat fitting is snug to the wood, the seam is soldered together. The mouth end of the brass is dressed to match the curvature of the end of the sheath and the ferrule. The throat piece will need a faceplate to finish it off. A piece of brass wider and longer than the end of the throat piece is scribed with a centerline. You will now need to scribe a line that matches the cross section of the base of your blade. It should be similar in appearance to the carved opening on the end of your sheath. When the pattern is scribed on your faceplate, drill a small starting hole for a jeweler's saw blade to fit in. You will be cutting out the center of your faceplate along the lines you drew. When your hole is cut, you will need to test fit it over the base of your blade. Use a flat jeweler's file to make any adjustments to fit the blade.

The faceplate is curved by lightly hammering it to shape and test fitting it with the blade in the sheath and the throat in place. When everything fits in place, scribe a line where the faceplate fits the throat. This line will guide you when soldering the faceplate to the end of your throat piece to assure that the blade opening is centered. Now solder the faceplate to the throat piece and trim off and dress down any excess brass and solder.

Each tip half is shaped by dishing (hollowing out or making concave) a piece of lead. Your goal is to create two half-cone shapes. I work back and forth between the lead block and the rounded horn of a small anvil made from a piece of crane rail. When you have your two halves closely shaped, test fit them on the end of your sheath. Typically they will be slightly oversized because of the uneven edges. The edges are dressed flat on a sanding disk or a flat piece of sandpaper. When the two halves are held together and fit snugly over the tip of the sheath and the edges line up with each other, the pieces can be soldered together.

Blade's Guide to Making Knives

Seating the throat on the sheath.

Cutting opening for the throat faceplate.

Each tip half is shaped by dishing into into a piece of lead.

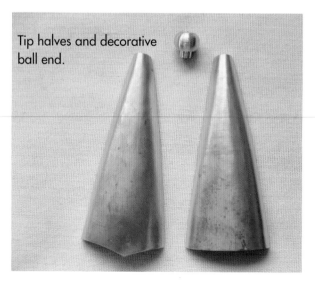
Tip halves and decorative ball end.

The suspension loop is soldered to the back of the throat piece.

A border design is cut in with a graver.

Smooth out your solder joints and edges and make sure the tip fits nicely over the end of your sheath. A decorative brass ball is made from a piece of 5/16-inch brass rod. I turn mine on a small metal lathe, but you could also file one to shape. I leave a little stub on one side of the ball that will sit inside the end of my tip fitting that I have ground even. Next you will solder the ball to the end of your tip fitting and file and sand it until it is smooth and even. Be sure to clean up any excess solder around the joint. Now wet sand both sheath fittings with 320-grit sandpaper to smooth out any hammer marks.

A suspension loop is made from 1/8-inch brass rod. Anneal about two inches of the brass rod and bend about 3/16 inch of one end at a right angle. Leave approximately 3/4 to one inch straight and then bend another right angle and cut off the excess beyond 3/16 inch. You should have a flattened "U" shape. This loop is soldered to the back of the throat piece near the lower edge. You will need to wet sand around the ends of the loop to clean up the solder joints and tarnish from the heat. I use a wedge-shaped sanding block and sandpaper to get

under the loop and around the post.

To dress up the final look of the fittings, a decorative borderline is scribed onto the face of the throat and tip, and cut in with a graver. All fittings are now wet sanded with 600 grit sandpaper.

Bookbinder's leather is what we use to cover the wooden sheath core. This type of leather is approximately 2mm thick, comes in many colors and textures, and is pre-finished. It is thin and flexible, and designed for contouring to decorative substructures. I draw a centerline down the back of my wooden sheath from throat to tip. This will be where the seam of the leather is. A good way to decide how wide the overall leather covering will need to be is to simply wrap the thin leather around your sheath leaving about 1/2 inch overlap along the back seam. The wooden sheath is laid on the backside center of the piece of leather and a line traced around it from the relieved area below the throat to about 1/2 inch from the tip.

It is better to have too wide of a piece than not to have enough leather to get a nice seam down the back. It is difficult to peel the leather off the wooden core once you have glued it down. Brush a thin layer of contact cement on the face of the sheath and on the traced centerline of your leather. When the contact cement is set, carefully place your sheath face down on the glued area of the leather. Flip it over and press it from the center out with the palm of your hand. Now, apply contact cement to one of the backsides of the remaining leather and also to the wood to which it will be glued.

Apply the contact cement up to the centerline that you have drawn. After the contact cement has set, start working the leather down onto the wood with your thumb. Work the leather from the face around to the back. You will need to work from the center towards the tip and in the direction of the throat to keep the leather even and prevent wrinkles. When the first side is firmly glued down onto the wood, you will need to clamp a straight edge from throat to point to line up with your centerline. Run a sharp knife along the straight edge and peel off the excess leather.

The gluing process is repeated on the second side. Be careful not to get any excess glue on the leather beyond your centerline. When your contact cement is set, work your leather down the same way you did for the other side. Your leather will overlap your centerline. Clamp your straight edge down on the overlap side of your centerline. Line the straight edge up with the cut edge of the lower layer of leather. Carefully cut along the straight edge being sure not to waver with your knife. If your cut is done well, you should have a nearly invisible joint when you peel the excess leather off.

If you have a design cut into the face of your sheath, you will now take a blunt pointed tool with a polished tip and press the leather into that design. Be sure to tool in the entire design.

On some of the later historical sheaths, the leather seam along the back was not stitched. The glue held the leather down to the core and the seams were nearly invisible. If you choose to use this method, you could use some colored wax-type shoe polish that matches your leather, working it into the seam. When it is buffed up with a cloth, you shouldn't see much of a line. For this project we will be using a stitched seam. The first step is to punch stitching slots along either side of the seam.

We use a four-slot leather punch and work our way from hilt to point. When you have all of your slots punched you will begin the stitching process. We use waxed nylon thread and two curved upholstery-type needles. Measure out the thread to four times the length of your seam. Thread a needle on either end and pass the needle through the two top slots at the throat end of your sheath and pull through until you have equal amounts of thread on each side of the seam. From that point, you will be stitching with the same sequence used to lace a shoe. When you get to the bottom of your seam, backstitch one slot and trim off the excess thread, leaving about 1/8 inch. Since I use nylon thread I heat the end of the thread with a lighter and press the melted end down against the sheath to seal the thread. When your sheath tip fitting is mounted it should cover the lower end of the stitching.

The leather is glued down.

Tooling the design on the face of the sheath.

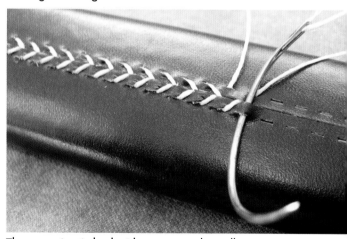

The seam is stitched with two curved needles.

## Assembly

Now we are ready to put everything together and make this into a finished knife. One last part that must be made is the tang nut. On many originals, this is nothing more than a flat, square nut about 1/8-inch thick and 1/2-inch square. You can get creative and filework this nut, or you can choose

Dirk hilt with antiqued fittings ready for assembly.

Pinning the side strap.

to make a round finial-type knob by drilling and threading a piece of brass rod. For this project we chose the simpler flat nut. It is cut from a 1/2-inch square, 1/8-inch thick piece of brass that I drilled a hole in the center of. The diameter of the hole will depend on what thread size you are tapping it with. Once the hole is threaded I contour the flat edges of the nut slightly with a half-round file.

The brass fittings are antiqued using a cold bluing solution. I choose to do this as it adds a vintage look to the dirk and eliminates the need to constantly polish the brass. I dip all of my pieces in a cold gun bluing solution and rinse them in water. When they are dry you can lightly buff them with a jeweler's rouge cloth.

All of the parts are laid out to make sure you have everything ready to mount. The first parts to mount are the side straps and ferrule. If you are using pins on your side straps you will need a small hammer and nail set. I run a thin bead of epoxy in the center of the channel of the wood where the side straps will sit. Line up and tap your pins lightly to set them. If your wood is a harder variety, you may want to pre-drill a pilot hole in the wood. Put a little epoxy inside your ferrule and press it into position to hold down the lower ends of your side strap. Now you can use your nail set to finish tapping your pins in. Next apply a little

epoxy to the inside of your pommel cap and press it in place with your solder joint to the back of your grip. Clean up any excess epoxy that might have squeezed out from around your fittings and allow your grip to cure.

Your blade will be the next step in the assembly process. You won't be using much epoxy as you are mainly trying to seat everything and keep it from twisting or rattling. Apply a little epoxy to the inside of the tang hole on the ferrule side and wipe any excess epoxy off the faceplate with alcohol. Slip the tang of the blade through the grip and thread your nut on the exposed end of the tang that is sticking through the pommel cap. Clean off any excess epoxy with alcohol and tighten the nut down gently.

I use the jaws of a wooden vise to tighten the nut so that I don't scratch my pommel cap or distort my tang nut. If you have too much threaded tang sticking out you can dress it down with a file or a belt grinder. One tip that helps is to cover your pommel cap with masking tape to prevent scratches while filing. When the epoxy is set you can now assemble the sheath fittings. Apply some epoxy to the exposed wood on the front and back face of the throat of the sheath where the fitting will cover. Do not put any epoxy around the blade opening.

Slide your throat fitting in place and slip the dirk

into the sheath. Clean any excess epoxy that has squeezed out of the bottom of your fitting. Apply some epoxy inside of the tip fitting down near the point, spreading it along the inside walls of the fitting and press the fitting in place. Pull the dirk out of the sheath and check for any epoxy that may have squeezed onto the blade from the throat fitting. If it looks clean, slip it back into the sheath and let the epoxy cure. If you will be wearing this dirk, you can make a leather belt strap that passes through the loop on the back of the throat fitting.

You now have a Scottish dirk you can say that you made yourself and hopefully this will be the beginning of many more adventures in Scottish folk art!

Completed dirk grip.

Completed dirk pommel.

The dirk is complete!

# Building a Damascus Locking-Liner Folder

## by Rick Dunkerley, ABS Master Smith

The first step in building a damascus locking-liner folder is choosing the design and the materials that will complement that design. For this project, I chose a large folding dagger. The symmetry of the pattern presents some challenges in material selection.

The damascus steel employed for this folder was a complex project in itself and could fill this chapter if described in complete detail. All of the patterns in the steel are based on "W's" patterns. The center stripe of Maltese cross-like patterns is an offshoot of one I saw on the Internet that had been done by Mick Maxen. Over a week of forge welding and 75 percent material loss went into the loaf of damascus from which these parts came. I felt this steel would complement the symmetry of the dagger design.

The folder also has black-lip pearl insets in the "picture frame" handle design. The picture frame handle technique is one of my favorites, as it adds a layered effect to the knife. For more layering, the knife also features a step-down design on the handle to create the illusion of the blade being too long for the handle of the folder. This is a technique that I first saw in the fabulous art folders of Rick Eaton.

Choose materials that will complement your design.

## Equipment List
Surface grinder
Milling machine
Drill press
Disc sander
2x72 TW-90 belt sander
2x72 Hard Core belt sander
Baldur buffer

## Materials List
3 pieces of damascus for blade and handle scales
2 pieces of 15N20 for liners
2 pieces of black-lip pearl for handle insets
1 piece of 416 stainless steel for back bar
6 0-80 Torx™ head screws for handle scales
3 1-72 slotted screws for back bar
2 1/16" hardened dowels for back bar
2 2-56 Torx head screws for pivot

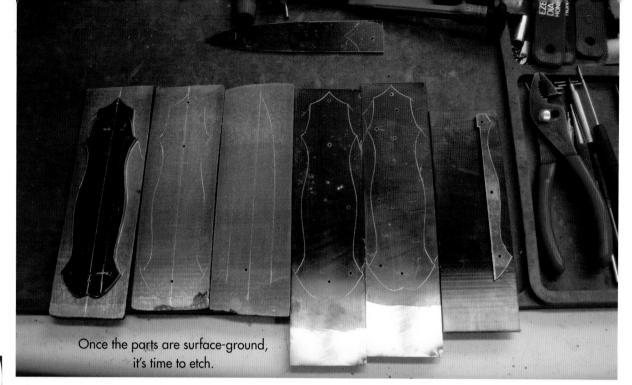

Once the parts are surface-ground, it's time to etch.

Laying out design to follow the pattern of the damascus.

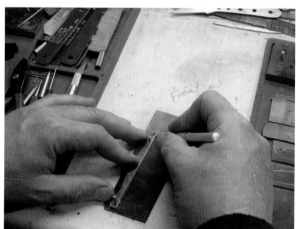

Scribing back bar pattern onto 416 stainless steel stock.

The first step in the actual construction of the folder is surface grinding the blade, back bar and handle scales. One side of the parts to be surface ground must be flat before the grinding. I use a disc sander to flatten one side until it will lay flat on the magnetic table of the surface grinder. A 50-grit belt is employed to grind the parts to .010 inch over the finished thickness, and then a 60-micron belt is used to grind to the desired thickness.

For this knife, the blade will be .100 inch thick. The back bar will be .118 inch thick to compensate for the .010-inch Teflon™ washers on each side of the blade. I know that .010 x 2 equals .020, but .018-inch oversize on the back bar helps to eliminate any side-play in the blade. The handle scales are ground to .125 inch thick.

With the parts surface ground, it is time to etch the damascus parts lightly in ferric chloride diluted with four parts water to one part ferric chloride. After etching, the damascus pattern is visible and will allow matching the blade pattern with the handle scales.

The folder pattern is used as a guide for where to drill all of the holes. It is critical that the drill press be set up with the table perfectly square to the chuck. It is also necessary to de-burr each hole so the part will lay flat on the table while drilling the next hole. For this knife, 0-80 screws will be the smallest used. The hole size for tapping 0-80 threads is a #55 drill bit, so that is the first size used to drill all the holes from the pattern. The pattern can be Super Glued to the material,

Using the pattern as a guide for where to drill all of the holes.

De-burring drilled holes on a disc sander.

Shaping the blade on a Milwaukee portable band saw. Note the use of a push block for safety.)

or tight-fitting pins can be used to keep the holes aligned.

After all of the holes are drilled with the #55 bit, the pattern can be traced onto the parts. The parts are cut out on the band saw. I have modified a Milwaukee portable band saw with a mounting bracket, table and foot pedal, and this little saw

Profiling handle scales with the small-wheel attachment on a TW-90 belt sander in horizontal position.

Tracing the bushing on small-wheel attachment.

Profiling blade on TW-90 belt sander.

Profiling back bar on TW-90 belt sander.

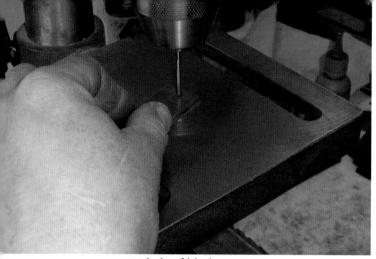

Ream pivot hole of blade.

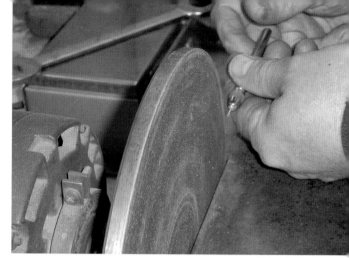

Turning heads of 0-80 Torx-head screws on disc sander.

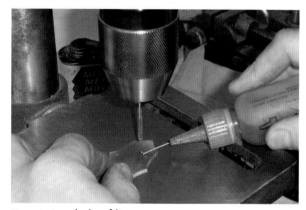

Ream pivot hole of liners.

Countersinking back-bar holes in left liner with #32 drill bit.

Checking countersinks for 0-80 screws on handle scales.

Parts all drilled and countersunk.

has cut out all of the folders I have ever made.

Next we grind the parts to the scribe lines from the folder pattern. After rough profiling, we turn the TW-90 belt grinder to the horizontal position and install the small wheel attachment. An aluminum bushing below the small wheel will follow the pattern while the belt grinds the part. When one side is ground, the part is flipped and the other side is ground.

The handle scales, liners, and back bar are ground using the tracer attachment. The back and bottom of the blade tang must be ground square on the 90-degree disc. These parts are finish-ground and symmetrical. The tracing bushing makes the symmetrical handle a snap. The versatility of the TW-90 belt sander allows special tooling like this to make many jobs much easier.

With all of the parts profiled, we drill all of the holes to the appropriate sizes. The handle scales will be drilled with a #55 drill, which is the clearance size for the 0-80 screws. The back bar holes on the left-side liner are drilled to 1/16-inch thick, which is the tap hole for the 1-72 screws used here. The left-side liner back-bar holes are drilled using a #49 bit—the clearance size for the 1-72 screws. The back bar is also drilled with the #49 bit. The pivot holes in the blade and liners are drilled with a #31 bit and then reamed with a 1/8-inch reamer.

Next, the clearance holes in the scales and liners will be countersunk for the screw heads. The #49 back-bar clearance holes on the left-side liner are countersunk with a #32 drill bit. I place a hardened steel block under the liner, and drill until the bit stops on the block. The heads of the 0-80 screws are turned down to .088 inch, and the handle scales are countersunk with a #43 drill bit.

Now the three #55 holes in the liners are tapped with a 0-80 tap. I use a hand-tap guide for the 0-80 size. Next, the three 1/16-inch back bar holes in the right liner are tapped with a 1-72 tap. I use a hand-tap guide for the 0-80 size. The three 1/16-inch back bar holes in the right liner are tapped with a 1-72 tap. Since I tap more 1-72 holes than any other size, I use an automatic reverse tapping head in my drill press for this size. I milled an aluminum block with a reservoir that holds tapping fluid so that the tap self-lubricates during the tapping operation.

Tapping 1-72 back-bar holes in right liner using a Tap-Matic.

Tapping 0-80 screw holes in liners with hand tap.

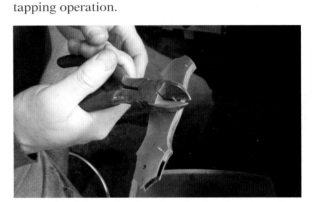

Cutting back bar screws to length.

Flushing back-bar screws on disc sander.

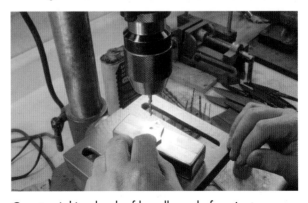

Countersinking back of handle scale for pivot screw heads.

With the tapping completed, the scales are screwed to the liners using the 0-80 screws. The extra length is cut off using side cutters, and the screws are flushed off on the disc sander. The liners and back bar are screwed together, and the screws are flushed off on the disc sander. The heads are also ground flush with the left-side liner. A foot pedal on the disc sander makes this and any flattening operations much easier, as the part can be held to the disc and then the pedal pressed for power.

The liner side of the handle scales must be countersunk to allow clearance of the head of the 2-56 screws for the pivot bushing. Once this is done, we can begin timing the folder in the open and closed position.

To begin the timing we install the full-length pivot bushing, and screw the scales onto the right-side liner. Next, the back bar is screwed to the right-side liner and the blade installed on the pivot. With the blade lying on top of the back bar, the blade is opened to the proper position and the back bar is scribed along the back of the tang. The blade is then closed, and the back bar is scribed along the bottom of the tang.

Since the damascus pattern of this knife is critical to the symmetry of the design, all material removed for timing the knife will be taken from the back bar. Once we are close to the scribed lines, the 90-degree disc is used to remove the final material. Now the blade and back bar should meet squarely in the open and closed positions. It is best to remove material slowly to avoid making a new back bar to replace one that is ground too short.

Now that the folder is timed, we will put the .010-inch Teflon washers on each side of the blade. The left-side liner and back bar are installed, and the excess length of the pivot bushing is ground flush on the disc. The result is a pivot bushing that is exactly the right length, and we didn't have to surface grind to get it. The 2-56 screws for the pivot will have to be shortened to allow complete tightening.

The knife is now disassembled, and the tang of the blade is ground at a seven-degree angle on the

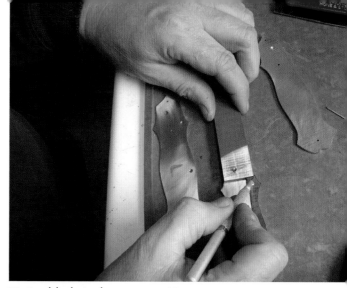

Timing blade in the open position.

Timing blade in the closed position.

The blade is timed and the knife is ready to make the pivot flush using a disc sander.

Squaring blade tang on disc sander.

Cutting the lock face using an air grinder and Dremel cut-off disc.

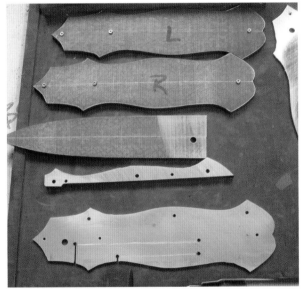

Face cut and second cut of lock done.

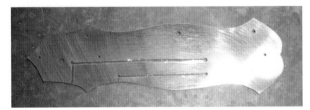

Lock cuts all completed.

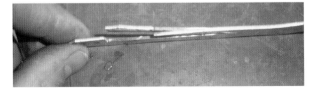

Lock bend done.

disc sander. The tang should be ground from about the top of the pivot hole to the bottom. The tang above the pivot hole is left-ground square so that it will mate squarely with the back bar.

The left side of the knife is assembled again, including the pivot and the back bar, and the blade is installed. With the blade held in the open position, a line is scribed on the liner along the lock cut. This will be the face of the lock cut. Next a line is scribed from the top of the face cut to make the lock itself. I like the lock to be at least two inches long, and prefer 2-1/4 inches.

This knife will have two more cuts to form a lock tab for a more pleasing look. At the ends of each cut, a 1/16-inch hole is drilled to relieve the liner and eliminate the sharp cut left by the Dremel cut-off disc. I use an air-die grinder to run the cut-off discs and can usually get the entire lock cut with three discs.

Before bending the lock, I surface grind the inside of the liners with an A-16 Trizact belt. This will speed up the finishing of the liners later on. Now we can bend the lock so that it will engage the lock cut on the back of the blade. I bend the lock with my hands, and prefer the bend to be at the end of the cuts. This makes for a smoother action than that of a shorter bend.

To check the lock engagement, we will put the right side of the knife together again and open the blade. If the face cut was made just ahead of the scribed line, the lock should not engage: this is what I want. The blade is now taken back to the disc set at a seven-degree angle, and a small amount of material is removed. This process is repeated until the lock is engaging nearly the entire thickness of the liner. This will allow the lock to wear yet still engage the blade tang solidly.

With the lock working correctly, we are now ready to install the detent ball. The blade is closed halfway, 90 degrees, and a line is scribed onto the lock along the bottom of the blade tang. The detent will be set between this line and the face of the lock.

The upper corner of the lock will allow the detent to work best so we center-punch as close to there as possible. I use a 1mm detent ball, so a #63 drill bit is used to drill the lock tab. I drill onto a hardened block and stop when the bit contacts the block. Now we set the detent ball using a small hammer and punch. The ball should be set down slightly more than half its diameter. With the detent set, the blade is put back on the half-assembled knife and closed fully several times. The ball will scribe an arc on the blade, and thus the recess where the detent ball will rest should be drilled slightly past the end of the arc. I like the recess to be .020-.030 inch above the arc.

I first drill with the #63 drill bit and close the blade to check if the detent ball falls into the recess. If not, I go to a slightly larger bit and enlarge the recess. This process is repeated until the detent ball complete falls into the recess.

Since the detent ball is protruding from the liner more than .010 inch, we will need to taper the lock slightly so that the blade will not be bound up while riding on the detent ball. To taper the lock, I lay the liner with the ball down on the magnet of the surface grinder. A .005-inch shim is placed under the ball, and the lock is ground until flush with the liner.

The knife can now be fully assembled, and the lock and detent checked for proper function. We should have a working locking-liner folder at this stage.

Now I will begin work on the blade. The bevels of the blade on this folding dagger will begin immediately after the step-down on the handle. This will make the step-down appear to be the ricasso portion of a normal blade, creating the illusion that the blade is too long for the handle.

A line is scribed along the step-down on both sides of the blade. Our bevels will begin at this line. I engraved this scribed line as an additional accent to the blade.

Next, a centerline is scribed on each edge of the blade. The rough grinding with a 2x72-inch TW-90 grinder begins.

Care must be taken not to remove too much material, or to grind over the centerline of the dagger blade. Once the rough grinding, using a

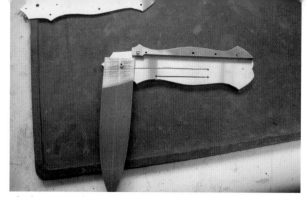

Blade opened 90 degrees to locate detent ball location.

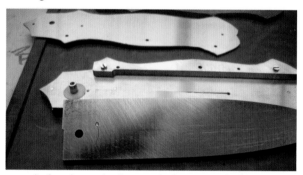

Drilling detent hole with #63 drill bit.

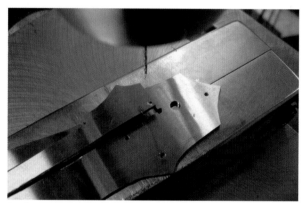

Dimple for detent ball at end of arc on blade.

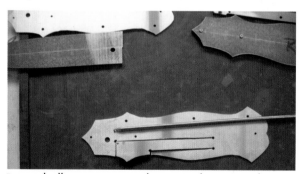

Detent ball on magnetized pin, ready to set in liner.

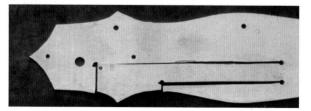

Detent ball set in liner.

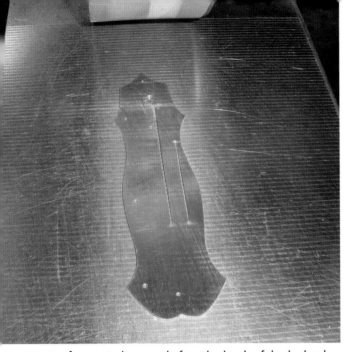

Surface-grinding a relief on the back of the lock tab.

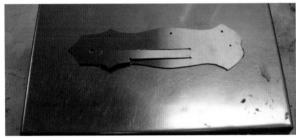

De-magnetizing the liner after surface grinding.

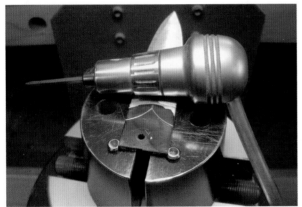

Lines engraved to follow step-down on handle scales.

Rough-grinding blade bevels on TW-90 belt sander.

Blade bevels filed to lines.

Blade tang checkered with checkering file.

Blade hand sanded to a 220-grit finish.

50-grit belt, is done, I go to a 120-grit belt and get closer to the finished bevels. The top edge of the folding dagger will not be sharpened, as it is not completely contained inside the handle. It can therefore be left a little thicker than the lower cutting edge. To finish the curved line along the step down, I use files and blend it into the ground portion of the blade. The centerline can also be straightened with the files if need be.

Because of the symmetry of this knife, no thumb stud will be used. Instead, a checkering file is employed on the top of the blade tang to provide purchase for the knife user's thumb to flip the blade open.

The folder blade is 1080-and-15N20 damascus that needs to be heat treated via the blade being brought up to 1,475°- 1,500° Fahrenheit in a high-

Blade's Guide to Making Knives

temperature salt pot. After a three-minute soak at that temperature, the blade is quenched in 120° hydraulic oil. I use hydraulic oil because I have a constant supply from servicing the equipment on our ranch. After the blade has cooled to under 100°, it is tempered at 425° for one hour. The tempering process should be repeated twice.

While the blade is tempering, the pockets for the black-lip pearl insets will be milled out of the inside of the handle scales. After applying Dykem blue layout fluid to the handle scales, dividers are used to scribe a line around the outside of the scales.

The black-lip pearl for these insets is about .078 inch thick, so the pockets will be milled .070 inch deep. I mill the pockets in two steps, taking .035 inch on each pass. This leaves a better finish to the pocket and allows the insets to lie flat.

With the pockets milled, we are ready to cut out the windows in the scales. The outside of the scale is coated with Dykem layout fluid and the dividers are opened wider than the inside pocket borders. This will ensure a lip left for the black-lip pearl insets to rest on. These windows will be simple ovals, and the mill is used to remove most of the material.

Once milled close to the line, the scale is clamped in a shoulder-filing jig, and files are used to clean up the scribed line.

When the windows are completed, the insets must be fitted to the pockets. I use tracing paper to make a pattern of the pockets and transfer that to the black-lip pearl.

The pearl is ground until a tight fit in the pocket is achieved. With the insets fit, I take the scales back to the surface grinder and grind the pearl down until it is flush with the inside of the handle scale.

Unless you work much faster than I do, the tempering cycles for the blade will be done by now. The blade can be sanded to a 600-grit finish and etched. The pivot area of the blade should be protected from the etchant by a resist coating. I use fingernail polish and cover the area on which the Teflon washers ride, and also cover the area that

Laying out windows in handle scales.

Milling pockets for handle insets in backs of handle scales.

Milling windows out of handle scales.

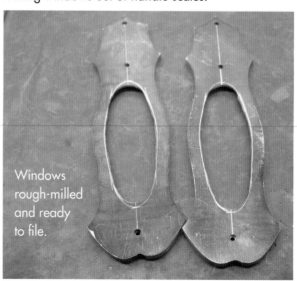

Windows rough-milled and ready to file.

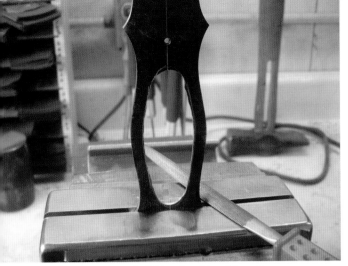

Filing windows held in shoulder-filing jig.

Blade hand sanded after heat-treating.

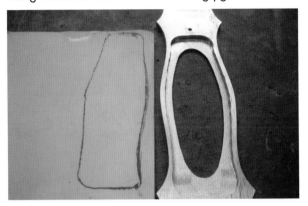

Making templates for handle insets.

Laying out step-down lines.

Surface-grinding the handle insets after fitting them.

Milling the step-down area.

the detent ball rides on. If this area is not protected, the detent ball will bounce along the highs and lows of the damascus pattern, and the action of the folder will not be smooth. I also resist off the back of the tang and the lock bevel of the blade.

The etching is done in ferric chloride mixed with warm water, 4 parts water to 1 part ferric chloride. I usually etch for 10 minutes and then rub with 2,000-grit sandpaper with a hard backing. Another 10-minute etching, and the blade should be finished. I use household ammonia to neutralize the etchant, and soak the part for at least 30 minutes. After neutralizing, the blade is again lightly sanded

with 2,000-grit paper. If everything looks satisfactory, the fingernail polish is removed with acetone and we have a finished blade.

Milling the step-down on the handle scales will be our next job. I used a circle template to mark the shoulder of the step-down on each handle scale.

Next, the scale is clamped on the table of the milling machine and the milling starts. I mill as close to the scribed line as I dare, and remove .080 inch in two passes. I'm sure a real machinist would have a way to mill this arc exactly, but I am not a real machinist.

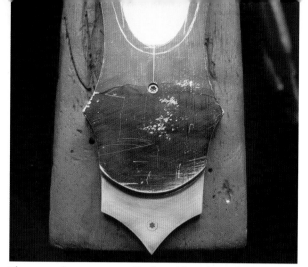

The step-down area is filed and hand sanded.

After the milling is completed, I use files to clean up to the line. Grinding the teeth off of one side of the file will prevent altering the flat step-down. After the filing is finished, the step-down is sanded to a 600-grit finish.

Now the knife can be completely assembled, and we will contour the sides of the handle scales. The contouring is started with a 120-grit belt on the 2x72-inch TW-90 belt sander. I like to have a nice, gradual dome from side to side, with no flat spot in the middle. The dome can then be cleaned up with a tight 120-grit slack belt, and then a 60-micron belt.

Before disassembling the knife, the edges of the handle can be sanded to a 600-grit finish. With the edges sanded, the knife is disassembled and the handle scales can be sanded. The sanding is done with 220-grit and then 400-grit sandpaper.

Before the 600-grit sanding, I engrave a highlight

line around the window on each scale. I also use a small file to round the edges of the window.

This creates a more pleasing effect than the square shoulders left after filing the window shape. After sanding the edges of the windows to a 600-grit finish, the scales are also sanded to a 600-grit sheen, and they are ready to etch. The etching is the same process as used for the blade.

Now we will turn our attention to the back bar. I file work the outside of the back bar in a simple, repetitive pattern—a simple pattern that complements the knife well. After filing, the outside is sanded to a 2,000-grit finish and polished on a

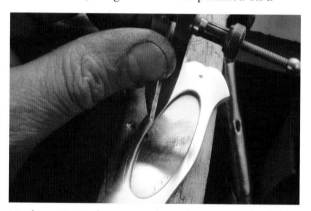

Marking accent line around window.

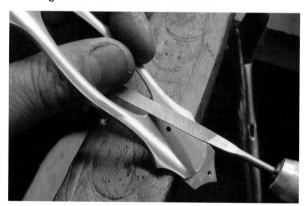

Beveling edges of window with needle file.

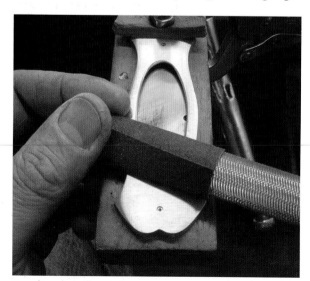

Sanding handle scales.

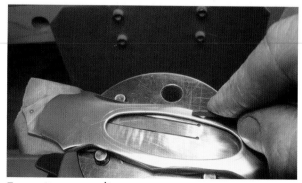

Engraving accent line.

File-working the back bar.

Sanding outside of liners.

loose buffing wheel with pink no-scratch compound.

The inside of the back bar is sanded to a 600-grit finish. I engrave my name in the center of the back bar and a simple running-leaf pattern around it. With the engraving done, 600-grit sandpaper is used to remove any burrs and the inside is now done.

The 15N20 liners are next. First the detent ball is driven out with a small, pointed punch. The detent ball is removed to avoid flattening it while sanding the liners. The insides and edges of the liners are sanded to a 2,000-grit finish. The outsides are sanded to a 600-grit sheen. After the sanding is completed, the liners are polished on a loose buffing wheel with pink no-scratch compound. After polishing, the liners are placed in an ultra-sonic cleaner to remove any polishing compound from the screw holes and filework. I usually clean the

liners for about 10 minutes in a solution of TSP cleaner and water.

Now the liners are ready to color in niter-bluing salts. The salt pot is heated on a propane burner until the salt is 600° Fahrenheit. The liners are hung in the molten salt on wires. I check the color until I have the color that I want. For this knife, I wanted the color to fade from purple to blue, and it worked out on the first try. The liners can be polished and re-blued if the color is not what was desired. During the bluing process, the liners will go from gold, to bronze, to purple, then to blue. The color change is discontinued, then, by quenching in warm water. After the liners cool, they are blown dry with compressed air and soaked in water-displacing oil.

After soaking for 30 minutes, the liners are dried with a soft rag and the detent ball reset and waxed with Renaissance Wax. The liners are now finished.

The three 1-72 screws that hold the liners and back bar together are fileworked while held in a pin vise. After the filework is done, the screw head is sanded with 600-grit sandpaper and polished.

The black-lip pearl insets are now sanded to a 2,000-grit finish and polished on the loose buff with pink no-scratch compound. The parts are ready to wax with Renaissance Wax. After waxing, the knife is ready for final assembly.

During the final assembly, light grease is applied to both sides of the Teflon washers and the resisted area on the blade. I also fill the detent dimple on the blade, which then lubricates the detent ball each time the knife is closed.

With the knife together except for the left-side

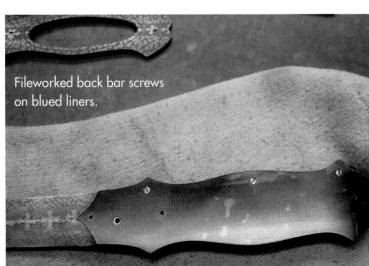

Fileworked back bar screws on blued liners.

liner, I check the lock engagement, detent function and the blade for side play. Everything should be fine, although the pivot bushing may need to be shortened slightly on the disc sander. The sanding of the liners sometimes makes this necessary. For me, blade side play is unacceptable. I would rather the knife's action be a little stiff than for it to have side play.

With the action as smooth as I want, the left side is installed and the knife is ready for Loctite. Before taking the handle scales off to access the pivot screws, the knife should be shaken to make sure the pearl insets don't rattle in the pockets. If they do, a few drops of Super Glue around the lip will hold them solidly.

With Loctite applied to the pivot screws, the handle scales are reattached and the knife is ready to sharpen. After sharpening, the knife is complete.

Hopefully you can sit back and enjoy the knife, and the process of making it. It is the process that interests me the most. The list of tools used to make this knife may seem lengthy, but the most important tool is persistence. Over 80 percent of the time taken to build the knife was handwork involving files or sandpaper. The machinery used makes some operations go more quickly, which is important for someone trying to make a living from fashioning knives. All of the operations could be done with hand tools—it would just require more time.

This is how I make a locking-liner folder. I'm sure there are other ways to do this same thing. I have simply developed a method that works for me. You may come up with techniques that work better for you in your shop.

# Lost Wax Casting for Guards & Pommels

## by Kevin L. Hoffman

Lost wax casting has been practiced around the world for more than 5,000 years. Known as a replacement process, the final product of the casting is actually a replacement for the original model that is burned away in order to create the finished part. The name is a bit of a misnomer because wax is not the only material that can be used to make the original model. Suitable materials include wood, plastic and any substance that can be completely vaporized at 1,250 degrees F, yet wax is the most widely used material for model making.

What makes this process so valuable in industry, and for us in knifemaking, is that it allows us to work in a soft and easily manipulated material that will later be replaced by any number of hard and durable materials to create the finished piece.

The author Kevin L. Hoffman.

Kevin Hoffman's "I Am The Walrus" features a damascus blade and walrus-oosic handle. He sculpted the walrus-head-and-tusks guard from wax and then lost-wax cast it in 7.5 ounces of sterling silver.

Wax is much easier to work with when we are designing and making our model than if we were to carve directly into gold, silver, copper or brass. This allows us to work faster and makes it possible to create parts that may be impossible to fashion any other way. It also gives us the ability to reproduce the piece many times if we choose by

Another example of lost wax casting is Hoffman's "Gent's Eagle" with a 14k-gold grip.

The waxes.

making a rubber mold of the model before the initial casting. Lost cast waxing gives us the ability to inject wax into a rubber mold to duplicate pieces in a large production run, in a small limited edition, or just as a safeguard against a failed casting.

Following are the methods and materials that I've found have worked for me in my shop over the years. Just like all aspects of knifemaking, there are real dangers associated with lost wax casting. It's important to read the safety information concerning the various materials and to exercise caution and safe shop practices at all times. Remember that you will literally be playing with fire. The use of safety glasses, protective clothing, respirators and proper ventilation is imperative and your responsibility.

## Wax on

There are five primary types of wax available from jewelry supply houses that are useful in the production of a model. Each has a unique working characteristic that lends itself to different types of model making, and it is not unusual to use more than one type in the process. Keep in mind that each individual manufacturer might use a slightly different color variation from other suppliers, so it is best to read each product description and not rely strictly on color when picking waxes.

First up is a purple sculpting wax with a melting temperature of 160 degrees F, but it is soft and easily manipulated by hand at body temperature, and thus easily formed. It is wonderful for making fast, rough models, but because of its high malleability

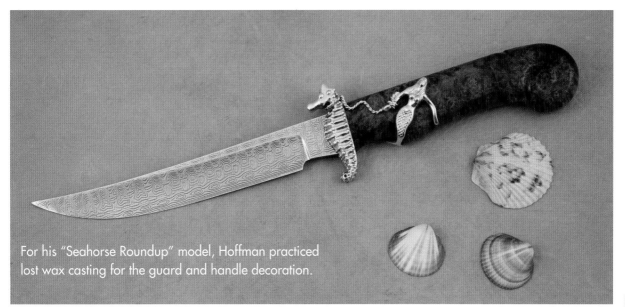

For his "Seahorse Roundup" model, Hoffman practiced lost wax casting for the guard and handle decoration.

and sticky consistency at body temperatures it is hard to get a nice, smooth surface finish when manipulated by hand. It picks up fingerprints and other blemishes easily. If kept cool after initial modeling it can be manipulated with wax working tools and smoothed out fairly effectively.

It is easier to get a nice, smooth finish in the winter or in a cool room because it warms to body temperature quickly and then gets sticky. Anything that helps keep it cool during finishing is a plus. It is extremely useful though when melted and used like hot glue for attaching other wax parts together and as a filler to smooth out joints when parts are assembled. I find this wax to be versatile and indispensable. Do not try to grind or use rotary burrs on this wax because all you'll end up with is a sticky mess.

Second is a blue wax that has only fair carving characteristics, and you must use sharp tools. It is semi-rubbery and flexible without being brittle, yet only hand finishes to a semi-smooth finish. It melts at 160-165 degrees F, but is formulated so that it can be handled and carved with hand tools without it becoming sticky. It is good for wax injection work in conjunction with a rubber mold when reproducing pieces because it exhibits medium flow characteristics, reproduces detail well and produces a smooth, flexible plastic-like surface finish when it cools. It has low shrinkage when injected, high memory and flexibility, and is a tough wax

that resists damage while handling. This wax is most often referred to as some variation of "Plast-o" or "Plasti-flex" wax. You can do some grinding and use rotary burrs on this wax, but it will load up and clog your tools and get gummy with very little friction.

Third is an aqua-green wax that is slightly harder than the blue, while still being semi-flexible, but it is not wise to bend or flex it too far because it will crack. It melts at 160-180 degrees F, however it can be handled and carved with sharp hand tools without it becoming sticky, will take a slightly smoother hand finish than the blue wax, and is stiffer without being rubbery. It is also good for wax injection work, cools to a smooth satin finish and reproduces detail well. I have found this wax to be a good base for modification.

I often make a rubber mold of a model at an intermediate stage of development when I have the basic shape and features established. I can then reproduce this base model and modify it while continuing to develop my finished design. This allows me to try design variations before selecting my final choice, or to develop derivative spin-off designs to create a series. This is a tough wax with low shrinkage, good memory, and good repair and modification properties. You can grind and use rotary tools on this wax also, but like the blue wax it will load up tools and belts quickly, and become gummy with aggressive friction.

Fourth is a dark blue/green hard wax—often described as turquoise—that is brittle and not at all flexible. It has a melting temperature of 155-160 degrees F, but is formulated to be hard and not at all affected by body temperatures. Designed for working with machine tools, the jewelry industry employs this style of wax for their CNC production design work. It can be drilled, milled or used with rotary cutting tools, like grinding burrs, and it can be shaped easily on a grinder. Like all waxes, it will load up tools, but this wax grinds to shape well and is easily cleaned from tools. Its working characteristics are much like plastic or hardwood, and it can be machined or carved with hand tools, gravers, files, scrapers, handsaws or power saws. And it sands to a fine finish.

It excels in a wax-injection capacity because it reproduces detail well and cools to a hard, shiny, smooth plastic-like finish with low shrinkage. This is the primary wax used in block form for carving into complex shapes with precise detail. It is easily cut using a coping saw, but it is brittle and will break if bent even slightly, so care is needed in handling and while working with it. The primary

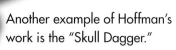

Another example of Hoffman's work is the "Skull Dagger."

tools for hand working this wax are files and scrapers.

Next on the list is a tan/yellowish wax that, when heated, becomes sticky, and is often referred to as "sticky wax." It has a melting temperature of 150-160 degrees F, but becomes flexible and somewhat sticky at body temperature. It is good for connecting dissimilar waxes together because it seems to stick to everything, yet when fully melted holds its heat for a long time, so care must be exercised when using it in conjunction with the other waxes. When employing it to connect other wax parts together, apply the minimum heat required to make it sticky enough to do the job. If you overheat this wax it has a tendency to soften or even melt the other waxes when you least want it to. It is flexible and holds its shape well when bent so I use it for sprues (holes and passages through which molten material is channelled into a mold), as well as for assembly work.

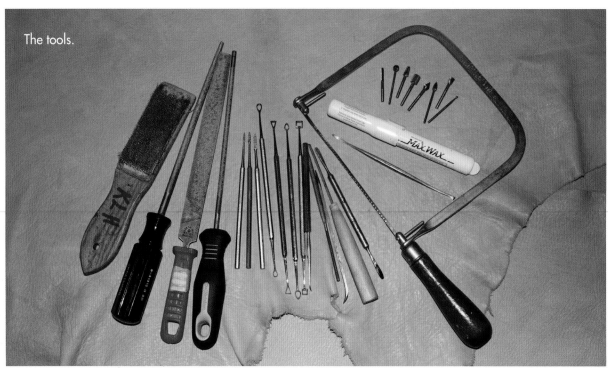

The tools.

These waxes are available in a variety of pre-made shapes, forms and sizes, from blocks and sheets to round or square wax wire, as well as wax pellets and specialty shapes expressly made for the jewelry industry. It is also easy to make your own sheets or blocks in whatever size or thickness you need by melting the wax down and pouring it into a pie tin or other form. After it has cooled it can be cut to shape.

## Wax-working tools

Although the purple wax can be easily worked by hand, all the other waxes require a variety of tools to effectively carve and shape them in any useful way. The purple, blue and aqua-green waxes are best worked with hand tools that look like modified dental instruments. You can buy them ready made from a jewelry supply house, or you can make many of them easily. A friendly dentist might give you his worn-out tools that you can adapt to great effect. Most of the tools for these waxes are a variation on the chisel or scraper because the waxes have a softer consistency that tends to clog up files, or cutting and grinding burrs.

Speedball makes and sells a line of carving tools designed for cutting linoleum and wood blocks for printmaking that also work well for carving wax. You can use a candle or an alcohol lamp to heat your hand tools for carving and smoothing the wax. Working these softer waxes is most akin to whittling. The hard turquoise wax can be worked with the hand tools, as well as all manner of files, cutting and grinding burrs, drills and power tools.

Scotch-Brite abrasive pads are great for doing surface smoothing and blending on your wax model. You can use a new pad for more aggressive smoothing or shaping, but it will leave substantial scratches in the wax. If you use a worn pad, it results in a nice, smooth finish with minimal residual scratches. There is one tool that is indispensable when working with all waxes—the "Max Wax Pen." It is a small handheld hot-wire tool that is used for spot welding, joining, smoothing, spot softening and adding wax to fill blemishes or gaps. It is most helpful for adding sprues to your finished model for casting.

## Model making

Although it is the most prevalent, wax is not the only material that you can use to make your model. If you create an intermediate rubber mold then you can use most any material you like. In the past I have employed wood, paper Micarta®, plastic model-car and airplane parts, seashells, and even interesting swizzle sticks. I am always saving unusual small items that I find for use as either reference examples or as pieces that could be incorporated directly into a model.

Once you have an idea of what to make, it is useful to sketch it full size for use as a consistent reference pattern for making parts. Once sketched, I start by cutting out and grinding my blade so that I establish the finished size of the tang and ricasso because I will be molding my wax directly

Preparing to make a block of wax for this project.

Pouring the wax.

around this area to get a good fit. For my guard and pommel I use the turquoise hard wax for this model. To make a suitable size block of wax from which to shape my guard, I line a small cardboard box with tin foil and spray it with a silicone mold release, pouring in the molten wax to the required thickness.

At the same time I pour wax into a plastic M&M candy container that I modified to make a cylindrical block from which I will later make my pommel. I've made wax blocks using pill bottles, plastic cups, brass tubing and many other odd containers to accommodate various design needs. Often I save odd-shaped containers just because they are an interesting shape or size, something that might come in handy for making a wax block or a silicone rubber mold.

After the wax cools, I cut out a block that is the right size for my guard. I start by making a hole in this block for my tang. First I drill a pilot hole or two in the wax where the tang will pass through. Next I heat the tang of my blade so that I can enlarge the tang hole by melting through with the heated tang itself. Do not worry, all these waxes melt below 200 degrees F, so there is no danger of harming your blade's temper by doing this.

Heating the tang.

Using the heated tang to melt through the wax block.

Wax blocks cooling.

Wax blocks ready to be worked.

Cutting the wax block with a hand saw.

Flattening and squaring the block.

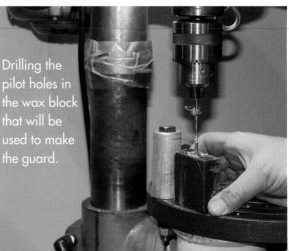

Drilling the pilot holes in the wax block that will be used to make the guard.

Fully seating the warm blade into the wax block.

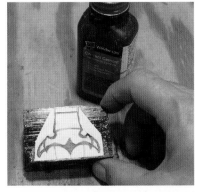

Applying the contact cement.

Affixing the full-size drawing of the guard to the wax block.

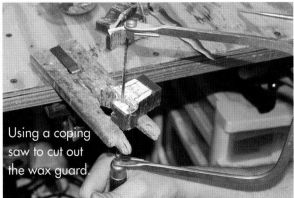

Using a coping saw to cut out the wax guard.

After I have melted the hole for the tang, and the seat for my blade is established in my wax block, I position a full-size copy of my guard drawing and attach it onto the face of the wax block. Contact cement does a nice job of adhering the drawing to the wax block, so brush a coat of the glue on the block of wax and the back of the paper pattern,

and let the glue dry for five minutes. After the glue is dry, position the pattern over the proper location on the wax block, but don't let the two surfaces touch until you are sure you have the pattern positioned correctly. Once that you are sure of the proper alignment, place the pattern on the wax so it sticks on contact. You won't be able to move it after it has made contact, thus the name "contact cement." Using a coping saw with a blade designed for wood (10 to 14 teeth to the inch), I rough cut the wax block to the shape of my guard.

Now it's time to start refining the model. Starting with coarse hand files smooth out the sides of the model, remove the ragged edges left by the saw and shape the model down to the outline of the pattern. At this point it is time to take the wax to the grinder. I use a 36-grit belt to shape the wax down close to its final dimensions so I can start

Using a coarse file to clean up and rough-shape the wax guard after cutting it out.

It fits and is starting to look like a guard.

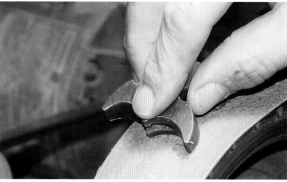

Going to the grinder and starting to refine the shape of the guard.

Starting the fine file work with a jeweler's file.

You can see that it grinds cleanly, but does load the belt up with wax.

Using a Scotch-Brite pad to smooth and shape the wax.

Back from the grinder to check the fit and get ready for hand shaping with files.

Starting the carving.

Here you can see that the files have loaded up with wax and are ready to be cleaned using the file card.

Using the Speed Ball cutting tool.

the final shaping with hand files and wax-working tools. No matter which wax is chosen (hard or soft), it will load up and clog the teeth of your files. This is to be expected and is easily remedied by the use of a stiff, short wired brush called a "file card." Brush across the rows of file teeth and clean them out periodically. The softer the wax or the finer the teeth on your file, the more often you will have to card/clean the file. Get used to it.

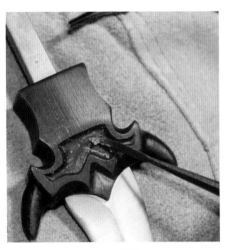

Refining the recess using my favorite cutting tool.

Ready to carve the next area.

Finished with the carving, sanding and smoothing.

# Preparing the mold

Once you have the carving of the model done it is time to add the sprues. In this case I'm using 1/4-inch wax rods of sticky wax to form the sprues and my Max Wax Pen to do the attachments. The sprues are the channels that will carry the molten metal into the void left when the wax is burned out. Remember this is a replacement process. The wax is only a placeholder for the metal that will replace it.

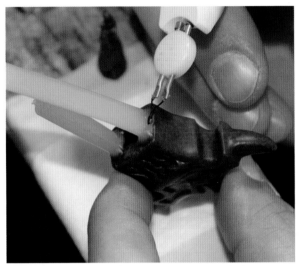

Using the Max Wax hot wire pen to attach the sprues to the bottom of the finished guard.

Placement of the sprues is one of the most critical aspects of lost wax casting. If you have too few sprues or they are not large enough to carry the volume of metal needed, or if they are not placed in the right locations to properly fill the mold, you will have a failed casting. Why is this critical? If the casting fails you have to start all over again because each mold is for one time use, and destroyed in the process of casting. Trust me a failed casting can ruin your whole day and probably your week, as well.

So with this in mind, what makes for good sprues? Sprues should be sized for the volume of metal that they will carry and they should be placed so that they feed the metal into the thickest portion of your model. They should be located in places that will not interfere with your design details. The idea is to facilitate the quick transfer of the molten metal into the void before it can start to cool and solidify. When evaluating your wax model for spruing, consider whether it has thin sections or is a large piece with small channels separating larger volume areas. It will often be necessary to add extra sprues to feed adequate metal into multiple high-volume areas or into thin sections that tend to cool and solidify fast.

For example, think of a barbell, if you only put one sprue at one end of a barbell you can not expect to flow enough metal thru the thin connecting tube to fill the other end before it cools and cuts off the flow of metal to the other end. In a case like that you need two sprues, one to each end of the barbell to get it to cast successfully. You also have to think about the path and flow of the metal as it courses into and through the mold. Even though the metal will be molten in liquid form, it is very dense, and like any liquid, it will flow best if it does not have to make sharp angles or U-turns, especially in the initial entry into the mold. You also want smooth radiuses without pinching or constriction, especially where the sprues attach to your model.

Constrictions in the sprues can cause turbulence in the metal flow and a porous casting with small voids or fractures. If attachment transitions are not smooth, it may result in small bumps or tabs of the investment plaster projecting into the sprue channels. Like plaque in your arteries, any small, thin plaster irregularities that project into the sprue channels can break off as the metal rushes past, and in turn, get carried into your mold. These small shards can potentially lodge in a part of the mold that will cut off the flow of metal and cause the casting equivalent of a heart attack—a failed casting.

At this point, when you have your sprues in place but before you attach the wax model to the sprue base and pour your plaster investment over the model, the model is weighed to determine how much metal will be needed to cast the part. The wax model for my guard weighed .32 troy oz., and the wax model for the pommel weighed .165 troy oz. I use the troy weight measurement because precious metals are traditionally measured and

Attaching the sprues to the sprue base. Notice the smooth, rounded transitions. This is important.

There are many standard sizes of sprue bases and casting flasks from which to choose.

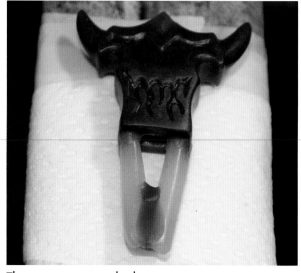

The sprues are attached.

sold in troy ounces. It really does not matter what measurement type you use, troy or grams, as long as you are consistent.

Because the weight of the metal will be much heavier than the weight of the wax model for the same volume, you'll need a formula to insure that you use enough metal to fill your casting and its accompanying sprues and sprue button. I'm using sterling silver for my guard and pommel so my formula for silver is this: the weight of the wax model with sprues attached, multiplied by 12.5 equals the weight of the silver I will need to cast my model with the appropriately sized sprue button. Using my formula .32 x 12.5 = 4 troy oz. is the weight of the silver I will need to cast my guard, and .165 x 12.5 = 2.0625 troy oz. of silver to cast my pommel.

The sprue button is formed by the semi-spherical protrusion in the center of the rubber sprue base that the wax model is attached to by the sprue. It plays several vital roles in the casting process. The first is that it forms the opening into

Weighing the wax guard.

Weighing the wax pommel.

the mold that acts as a funnel to direct the molten metal up the sprue channels into the mold. Second it acts as a reservoir for excess metal to insure that you have a full casting, and it holds heat, thus keeping the metal inside the mold at molten state for a longer period of time. While the metal is in a molten state and the casting is spinning, it provides added weight to the centrifugal force, driving the molten metal into the mold and filling out all areas of your casting to insure the greatest possible detail is achieved.

I'm using 2-1/2-inch diameter x 4-inch tall casting flasks for my molds this time, but there are many standard sizes on the market from which to choose. The only limitation is the capacity of your casting machine, and mine can handle flasks up to 3-1/2-inch diameter x 5 inches tall, which is fairly standard. The sprue button is built into the flexible rubber sprue base and varies in size in proportion to the size of the flasks and their capacity. For small shop casting machines like mine, the sprue buttons are generally all about the same size and will create a sprue button of about one troy ounce.

## Silicone rubber mold

At this point you have finished your wax model, attached the sprues and weighed it to establish the proper weight of the metal you'll need for each of your castings. Before you attach it to the sprue base, this is the time to decide if you want to make a silicone rubber mold of your finished wax model. Remember, if for any reason the casting should not be successful, your wax model will be destroyed in the casting process. For this reason, especially with the complex difficulty of carving models, I often make a silicone rubber mold so that in the unlikely event that my casting fails I can quickly reproduce my wax model and try again with minimal pain and loss of time.

I use a room temperature, vulcanizing, two-part silicone molding compound that cures overnight. I attach my model to a mold frame that I will fill with the silicone-rubber molding compound. I'll be pressurizing it overnight using the same technique that I describe fully in the section about making

Preparing the mold frame to make a silicone rubber mold of the finished wax guard.

The mold has been allowed to set overnight, and we see the wax model encased in the cured silicone rubber mold.

The closed-up mold frame.

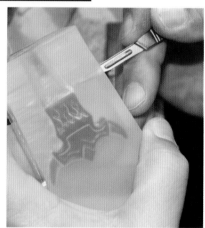

Carefully cutting the silicone mold open using a scalpel and a zigzag cut.

Ready to pour in the silicone.

The finished silicone rubber mold ready just in case I need it.

the plaster molds for casting. After your silicone mold has cured, you cut it open with a scalpel or Exacto knife using a zigzag cut to free and retrieve your original wax model. The purpose of the zigzag cut is to create an integral keying mechanism so that when your rubber mold is closed back up for wax injecting it will automatically align itself properly. Now you have a perfect negative space that will, when injected with molten wax, reproduce your original wax model. You can cast with the security that if something should go wrong

with your casting, you don't have to start back at scratch and re-carve your model.

After cutting open your rubber mold, retrieve your wax model, repair any nicks you may have made while freeing it and attach the wax model to a rubber sprue base in preparation for pouring the final plaster mold. I use the purple soft wax for this—the same wax I use to attach and smooth my sprues. After attaching your model to the sprue base, slip the base onto a steel casting flask and wrap the top with a ring of masking tape with half

It's important that the wax models fit properly in the flask and don't touch the sides.

Starting the mixing with the dry investment plaster.

Adding the water a bit at a time.

Mixing by hand is the best way to make sure you get all the lumps out.

The perfect consistency is like pour-able sour cream.

its width above the lip of the flask. This creates a dam so that the flask itself can be filled all the way to the top with plaster.

It is important that your wax model not touch the sides of the flask. I like to leave 1/4" clearance between the model and the inside of the flask to insure a successful casting. It is also important that there is at least 1/2-inch plaster covering the top of your model so the weight of the metal doesn't break through the bottom of your plaster mold when it is spun with great force during the casting process. The last thing you want is molten metal spewing from the bottom of your mold during casting.

For my investment plaster I prefer Kerr Satin Cast 20. To start the investment process, scoop enough investment powder into a rubber mixing bowl and slowly add water while mixing until it has the consistency of pour-able sour cream. I mix my investment by hand so that I can get the best feel for its consistency, and to make sure that all lumps have been eliminated and all dry powder has been mixed in fully. You have about a 10-minute working window after you mix your plaster before it becomes too stiff to use.

Once the plaster is the right consistency, tilt your casting flask so that you can slowly pour the investment down the inside of the flask and not directly onto the wax model. You don't want to dislodge it or break off the sprue from the base or your wax model. Once the investment has flowed up and covered your model, fill the flask all the way to the top. The masking tape dam will contain any overflow and insure that you have a full flask. Any excess will be trimmed off after the plaster has set. At this point there will be thousands of tiny air bubbles trapped in the investment that, if not removed, will stick to your model, covering the finished casting with small metal bubbles that will mar the surface and need to be filed off later. You really don't want that. There are several methods and products designed to deal with these bubbles, but the two steps that I've found to be the most effective in eliminating this problem are vibration and pressure.

I've marked what's inside, the weight of the wax piece and the weight of the metal needed for casting.

The full flask is vibrated on top of the compressor housing until you can see the bubbles coming to the top.

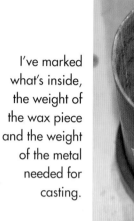

The masking tape dams are in place.

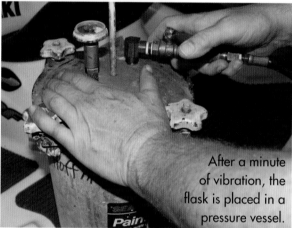

After a minute of vibration, the flask is placed in a pressure vessel.

Pour the investment plaster down the side of the flask.

The flask is pressurized with compressed air to 45 psi (pounds per square inch).

The flask is full.

Immediately after filling the flask I place it on top of my air compressor housing and turn on the compressor to vibrate the flask while it builds up air pressure for the next step. After a minute of vibration I place the flask in a pressure vessel and pressurize it with compressed air to a pres-

After 10 minutes in the pressure tank, remove the tape.

Trim off the excess plaster.

Marking the plaster with what's inside.

Removing the rubber sprue base.

Sprue bases removed and ready to dry overnight.

"G" for guard and "P" for pommel clearly inscribed into the plaster.

sure of 45 psi (pounds per square inch). When the wet investment plaster is pressurized above 35 psi, the bubbles are forced back into solution and eliminated almost entirely. Leave the flask under pressure until the plaster sets, about eight to ten minutes. You may still get one or two stubborn bubbles from time to time, but you won't have the chicken pox effect that can plague you without this step. My pressure vessel is a pressure tank that I salvaged from a paint sprayer rig, but you can buy one for about $80 from Harbor Freight if you can't find a used one.

Once the plaster has set, remove the masking tape from the top of the flask, and using a knife, remove any excess plaster back down to the top of the flask. Immediately scratch into the damp plaster something that will tell you what part is in the flask. This is critical because if you are burning

out more than one flask you will need to be able to identify which part you are about to cast and how much metal you will need for casting that flask. Believe it or not, once you cover the wax models with plaster they all look the same.

If you mix enough plaster to invest two flasks at the same time, mark the outside of each flask with what's inside on masking tape on the outside of each flask. That way when you pull them out of the pressure vessel you'll know what to scratch into the damp plaster. Trust me, after all the work you've done to get to this point you don't want to be guessing which flask has what piece! Now carefully remove the rubber sprue base from the flask and set the flask aside to dry at least overnight, but not longer than 48 hours because you want some moisture left in the investment when you start the burnout cycle.

# The burnout

A burnout cycle can take from three to eight hours depending on the number and size of the flasks in the kiln. When loading the kiln, place the flasks with the opening down and sitting on a wire rack or grid so that the melting wax and fumes can escape. I use a heavy woven-wire mesh grid that fits into a steel tray so that the wax can get out easily, but is collected in the tray and doesn't flow out of the kiln or soak into the fire brick of the kiln. There's no wax mess this way. I have a kiln with a digital controller and built-in pyrometer so I'm able to accurately and easily set my temperatures to do my burnouts in five stages.

Stage #1: Starting out slowly I set the kiln to 200 degrees F and let it soak for an hour or two to warm the flasks all the way through. This will melt out the majority of the wax and slowly drive out the moisture in the investment. It's important to start out so slowly because you don't want to create steam pressure in the investment before you've softened and melted most of the wax out of the cavity. Until you have eliminated most of the wax from the mold, creating steam would risk fracturing the investment plaster.

Stage #2: Now you can turn the kiln up to 400 degrees so that the remaining moisture will turn to steam and help to evacuate the wax further. Let it stabilize at heat, then soak for half an hour.

Stage #3: Now you can turn the kiln up again to 800 degrees and let it stabilize and then soak for half an hour again.

Stage #4: Turn the kiln up to 1,000 degrees, let it stabilize and soak for half an hour.

Stage #5: Turn the kiln up for the last time to 1,250 degrees, and let it stabilize and soak for half an hour while you get the casting machine ready.

At 1,250 degrees the wax is totally vaporized, and you will have a mold that is ready to cast. If you have a kiln that you know overrides or a pyrometer that you don't trust, be careful at this stage to keep the temperature below 1,350 degrees F. At 1,350 degrees F the binders in the investment start to break down, weakening the mold and also releasing sulfur into the mold that will degrade the

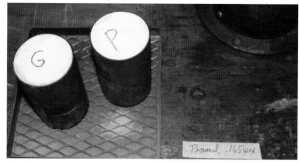
Flasks placed sprue bottom down on the wire rack.

Loading the tray into the kiln.

You can start to see some of the wax melting out of the mold.

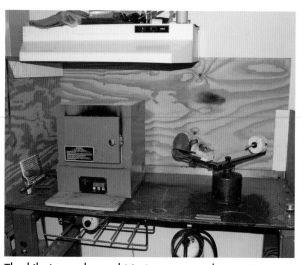
The kiln is ready, and it's time to start the casting.

quality of your casting. If you are casting multiple flasks you can turn the kiln down to 1,000 degrees to maintain a good working temperature for the flasks while they wait their turn for casting, and thus eliminating any risk of overheating the molds.

# The casting

I use a hand-wound, spring-loaded, Broken Arm Centrifugal Casting Machine. These machines are a mainstay in most small jewelry shops and metal studios. They get their name "Broken Arm" because of the part of the casting arm that holds the mold. The crucible starts out bent at a 90-degree angle to the counterweight portion of the casting arm, resembling a broken arm supported in a sling. The purpose of this misalignment at the start allows the molten metal to be thrown straight back into the forcing cone of the crucible, funneling it directly into the sprue button of the mold. Then

The Broken Arm Centrifugal Casting Machine is wound up and locked in the starting position.

Preheating the crucible.

the arm straightens out so that centrifugal force added to the weight of the metal drives the metal into all the crevices and details of your model while holding the molten metal into the mold until it cools enough to solidify.

Before you pull a flask out of the kiln and place it in the machine, wind the machine two or three turns, depending on the amount of metal you are using, and set the stop trigger. Now preheat the crucible before you add any metal and before you put the flask in the cradle. This does two things for you, first it will speed the melting and casting process considerably, and it will keep the mold flask from cooling off too much while the metal is melting. Once you have the machine wound and the crucible hot, pull a flask from the kiln with tongs, place it in the cradle and slide the crucible up against it to hold it in place.

I wrap a wire over the top of the flask, securing it to the cradle as a safeguard against it shifting or coming loose during casting. Not everyone does this, but I find it helpful. Now put the pre-measured metal that corresponds to the flask that you are casting into the crucible and melt the metal. When the metal looks molten, right before I cast, I check to insure that it is melted completely. Using a titanium rod that has been dipped in borax, I stir the molten metal, checking for any lumps that may not have melted yet. The borax acts as a flux, cleaning and floating any impurities in the molten metal to the surface and off onto the side of the crucible so that they don't end up in your casting.

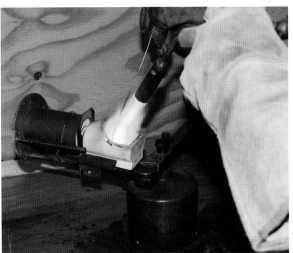

Fluxing the molten silver.

Final check of the metal, and three, two, one …

Go! The casting is halfway through the first revolution.

Into the second revolution, and the arm is fully extended.

A full sprue button, and a successful casting so far.

Set the hot flask aside until all the red is gone from the sprue button.

When the metal is up to heat and completely molten, release the stop pin and check the metal one last time to make sure it is ready. If all is still ready, simultaneously release the arm to spin while removing the torch flame from the crucible of molten metal, and stand back to let it spin. Even though you will be anxious to see how your casting has turned out, don't stop the spinning prematurely. Let it spin down to a stop to insure that the metal doesn't run right back out of the mold because you didn't give it enough time to let the sprue button harden sufficiently.

Once the arm spins to a stop, grab the tongs and slide the crucible forward to remove the flask from the machine. Set the flask aside on a fire brick to cool until there is no visible red left and the sprue button has turned black, about five minutes, but not much longer. When I'm casting multiple flasks, after casting a flask, I set it aside to cool while I cast the next flask, and by the time I finish casting the subsequent flask, the first is ready to quench.

With tongs, hold the hot flask horizontally and submerge it into a bucket of water. It's important to quench the flask horizontally because it will spit and sputter violently, and this directs any hot splatter away from your face and body. The flask will still be extremely hot, and this will help you by boiling the plaster out of the flask and off of your casting, making it easier to clean off your finished casting.

If you let the flask cool too much before quenching, it won't boil sufficiently and you would have to chisel the investment out of the flask, possibly damaging your casting. You don't want to do that! So, if for some reason you get distracted and let a

Quenching the flask.

Blade's Guide to Making Knives

flask cool too long, don't despair and don't dunk it yet. Instead put it back into the kiln and reheat it before you dunk it. This isn't optimal because it can cause excess oxidation to form on the metal, but it is much better than chiseling out the investment.

After the flask stops boiling and sputtering in the bucket you can fish your finished casting out of the water. To clean any remaining plaster off of the casting, I use a wooden pick made from a sharpened chopstick and a brass wire brush. These will make short work of cleaning the casting, but neither of which will damage your casting. Check out the piece to make sure it cast properly and admire your handiwork. Toss it into a pot of dilute acid called "pickle" (I use Sparex 2) to clean and remove any oxides that may have formed in the casting process.

Checking out the finished casting.

Start the cleanup with a sharpened chopstick.

Then use a brass brush.

The beautiful, clean, finished castings. Notice a couple of small, stubborn bubbles.

With the sprue buttons removed, the finishing process is started.

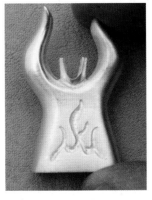
I've solded the setting into the pommel for the 6mm ruby, as well as tapped and threaded it to fit the tang screw.

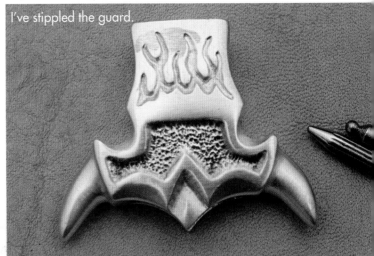
I've stippled the guard.

Side view of the tang screw coupling.

Top view of the tang screw coupling.

All the semi-finished parts are ready to assemble.

At this point you can see my finished castings with the sprues still attached. You can also spot a couple of stubborn little bubbles that hung on despite my best efforts to eliminate them. These few bubbles are no big deal and they are easily removed, but without the vibration and pressure treatment these beautifully clean castings could have been covered with hundreds of bubbles. Using a jeweler's saw, cut off the sprues and you are ready to finish the casting so that it is ready for assembly with the rest of the parts to finish your knife. I use my flex-shaft grinder along with Cratex rubberized abrasive points to do a lot of the finishing. I also use a Scotch-Brite belt on my grinder for smoothing and finishing before polishing. I'll be setting a 6mm ruby into the pommel of my dagger so at this point you can see that I've soldered the setting for the stone into the top of the pommel. I've also used some stippling punches to create a pebble grain surface in the recesses of the guard.

On hidden-tang knives I always thread my pommel for strength in the finished knife and so that I can draw all of the pieces tightly together during final assembly while the epoxy sets. I've never liked to thread the end of the tang itself for several reasons. First is because it limited my ability to vary the length of a handle after the blade was heat treated if I decided to switch handle materials or for any other unforeseen reason. The second is because some materials, like a curved piece of stag, can give you alignment problems.

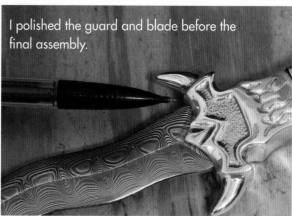

I polished the guard and blade before the final assembly.

All the parts have been assembled and glued into place.

Third, with expensive blade steels like stainless damascus, I don't want to hide more expensive steel under the handle than is structurally necessary, but I don't like to weld a plain-steel tang to a damascus blade just beyond the guard either. So to solve all these problems I came up with this neat solution by making a coupling to join my two-thirds length tang to a threaded rod that can be any length that I need and it can also be angled up or down to accommodate any handle curvature that I need.

The finished guard casting weighs 2.355 troy oz., and the finished pommel casting weighs .945

The finished product.

troy oz. You can see that the sprues and sprue button comprises about one third of the total weight of the metal needed to make a successful casting. Don't worry there is no waste. The sprue buttons will be reused for another casting in the future. When you are using metal that has been cast before, it is best to mix it half to half with new casting grain on each subsequent casting for best results. Fluxing the molten metal with borax just before casting also helps eliminate any residual impurities from previous castings.

Now I have all of my semi-finished parts made, but before I assemble them I'll polish my blade and the lower half of my guard with all its nooks, crannies and projections where the blade and guard seat together. I'm doing this because these areas will be almost impossible to adequately polish completely if I don't do it before assembly. It's time to rivet my tang extension in place, mix my epoxy and assemble all the parts. After the epoxy has set I've gone back to my grinder to smooth out all my transitions, guard to handle, handle to pommel, to an 800-grit finish before doing my finish polish and inspection. Now all that's left to do is clean off any buffing compound residue, set the stone, sharpen the blade and take the final pictures.

That's Lost Wax Casting and that's how it's done.

# Product and supplier reference list

www.riogrande.com
www.fdjtool.com
www.HarborFreight.com

# About the author

Kevin graduated from The University of Iowa with a master's degree in studio art —Jewelry & Metalsmithing.

He has been a knifemaker for 30 years, a member of the Knifemakers' Guild since 1983 and was elected to the Board of Directors in 2007. He is an Adjunct Professor at Armstrong Atlantic State University in the Department of Art, Music & Theatre, where he teaches Art Appreciation, 3-D Design and Jewelry & Enameling.

Web site: www.KLHoffman.com
E-mail: kevh052475@aol.com
Phone: (912) 920-3579

# Add to Your Smithing Skills with More Books from **BLADE**

## WAYNE GODDARD

### The Wonder of KNIFEMAKING

**THE WONDER OF KNIFEMAKING · 2ND EDITION · GODDARD**

2nd Edition

**Learn from the Master**
- Steel Selection
- Heat Treating
- Testing Performance

Whether you've been making knives all your life, or you're just learning the ropes, there's no better source for valuable and reliable advice than Wayne Goddard. Now, years of questions from fellow knifemakers and detailed answers from Goddard are in one easy-to-follow book. In the Wonder of Knifemaking you'll gain valuable instruction about every facet of knifemaking, from selecting the steel to finishing the blade. Plus, you'll discover tips, tricks and techniques that you can put to use right away.

Item# X3269 • **$27.99**

## Bladesmithing with Murray Carter

**Modern Application of Traditional Techniques**

In this popular new book, knifemaking phenom Murray Carter shares the details of revered and often mysterious, traditional Japanese knifemaking techniques.

Through Carter's easy-to-follow instructions you'll learn traditional Japanese techniques and the steps for using these techniques with modern knifemaking applications. This is one knife book you'll read again and again.

Item# W1852 • **$27.99**